strange now to think of you, gone without corsets & eyes,

while I walk on the sunny pavement of Greenwich Village

downtown Manhattan, clear winter noon, and I've been

up all night, talking, talking, reading the Kaddish aloud,

listening to Ray Charles Blues shout blind on the phonograph

the rhythm the rhythm — and your memory in my head three years

after — And read Adonais' last triumphant stanzas

aloud — wept, realizing how we suffer —

And how Death is that remedy all singers dream of, sing,

remember, prophesy as in the Hebrew Anthem, or the

Buddhist Book of Answers — and my own imagination

of a withered leaf — at dawn —

Dreaming back thru life, Your time — and mine accelerating toward Apocalypse,

the final moment — the flower burning in the Day

Dreaming back thru life, & other time, all time's other time,

your time — and mine accelerating toward Apocalypse,

the final moment, last look at the burning flower in the

unfathomed blue Day —

And what comes after, looking back on that, back on the

mind itself that saw the star's night's city,

+ flash away, and the great dream of Me or China,

or you and a phantom Russia, or a crumpled bed

that never existed —

in the Dream, Trapped in its disappearance,

Sighing, screaming with it, believing it All, buying &
selling pieces of Phantom, worshipping each other

Worshipping the God included in it all — longing or
inevitability? — while it lasts, a vision — anything
more?

while it laps about me, as I go out and walk the street,
look back over my shoulder, 7th avenue, the
battlements of window office buildings shouldering
each other together high, under a cloud, tall as the
sky an instant — and the sky above, a bleak
blue voiceless place,

or down the avenue to the South as I walk toward
the lower East side — where you walked 50
years ago, little girl — from Russia, eating the
first poisonous tomatos of America — frightened
on the doch —

then struggling in the Crowds of orchard Street
Toward what — Toward Newark ___

Toward Candy Store, first home made sodas of
the Century, hand Churned Ice Cream in backrooms

KADDISH

AND OTHER POEMS
1958–1960

ALLEN GINSBERG

Afterword by Bill Morgan

'—Die,
If thou wouldst be with that which thou dost seek!'

CITY LIGHTS BOOKS

Grateful acknowledgment is made to Peter Hale of the Allen Ginsberg Trust
for permission to reproduce Allen Ginsberg's photographs, facsimile pages from
the original draft manuscript, the essay, "How Kaddish Happened," and Naomi
Ginsberg's portrait of Allen Ginsberg.

Library of Congress Cataloging-in-Publication Data

Ginsberg, Allen, 1926-1997.
  Kaddish and other poems : 1958-1960 / Allen Ginsberg. — 50th anniversary ed.
    p. cm. — (The pocket poets series ; no. 14)
  Includes a new afterword along with previously unpublished family photographs, his
      mother's paintings, and documents and letters relating to the composition of
      the poem.
  ISBN 978-0-87286-511-2
  I. Title.
  PS3513.I74K3 2010
  811'.54—dc22
                              2010038347

Vist our website: www.citylights.com

City Lights Books are published at the City Lights Bookstore,
261 Columbus Avenue, San Francisco, CA 94133.

Dedicated
to
Peter Orlovsky
in
Paradise

'Taste my mouth in your ear'

Note: Magic Psalm, The Reply, & The End *record visions experienced after drinking Ayahuasca, an Amazon spiritual potion. The message is: Widen the area of consciousness.*

—A.G.

Acknowledged, the established literary quarterlies of my day are bankrupt poetically thru their own hatred, dull ambition or loudmouthed obtuseness. These poems were printed in *Yugen, Combustion, Liberation, Beatitude, Playboy, Big Table, Evergreen Review, Jargon 31, New Directions 17, The Outsider, New Departures, Jabberwock (Sidewalk), Poetry London-NY* and strangely the *London Times Literary Supplement.* Most of these publications started in the last half-decade, two were begun by youths who quit editing university magazines to avoid hysterical academic censorship.

—A.G.

(Dated 1961)

CONTENTS

KADDISH

For Naomi Ginsberg, 1894–1956

I

Strange now to think of you, gone without corsets & eyes, while
     I walk on the sunny pavement of Greenwich Village.

downtown Manhattan, clear winter noon, and I've been up
     all night, talking, talking, reading the Kaddish aloud,
     listening to Ray Charles blues shout blind on the
     phonograph

the rhythm the rhythm—and your memory in my head three
     years after—And read Adonais' last triumphant stanzas
     aloud—wept, realizing how we suffer—

And how Death is that remedy all singers dream of, sing,
     remember, prophesy as in the Hebrew Anthem, or the
     Buddhist Book of Answers—and my own imagination of
     a withered leaf—at dawn—

Dreaming back thru life, Your time—and mine accelerating
     toward Apocalypse,

the final moment—the flower burning in the Day—and what
     comes after,

looking back on the mind itself that saw an American city

a flash away, and the great dream of Me or China, or you and
     a phantom Russia, or a crumpled bed that never
     existed—

like a poem in the dark—escaped back to Oblivion—

No more to say, and nothing to weep for but the Beings in the
     Dream, trapped in its disappearance,

sighing, screaming with it, buying and selling pieces of phantom,
     worshipping each other,

worshipping the God included in it all—longing or inevita-
bility?—while it lasts, a Vision—anything more?

It leaps about me, as I go out and walk the street, look back
over my shoulder, Seventh Avenue, the battlements of
window office buildings shouldering each other high,
under a cloud, tall as the sky an instant—and the sky
above—an old blue place.

or down the Avenue to the South, to—as I walk toward the
Lower East Side—where you walked 50 years ago, little
girl—from Russia, eating the first poisonous tomatoes
of America—frightened on the dock

then struggling in the crowds of Orchard Street toward what?
—toward Newark

toward candy store, first home-made sodas of the century, hand-
churned ice cream in backroom on musty brownfloor
boards—

Toward education marriage nervous breakdown, operation,
teaching school, and learning to be mad, in a dream—
what is this life?

Toward the Key in the window—and the great Key lays its
head of light on top of Manhattan, and over the floor,
and lays down on the sidewalk—in a single vast beam,
moving, as I walk down First toward the Yiddish
Theater—and the place of poverty

you knew, and I know, but without caring now—Strange to
have moved thru Paterson, and the West, and Europe
and here again,

with the cries of Spaniards now in the doorstoops doors and
dark boys on the street, fire escapes old as you

—Tho you're not old now, that's left here with me—

Myself, anyhow, maybe as old as the universe—and I guess
that dies with us—enough to cancel all that comes—

What came is gone forever every time

That's good! That leaves it open for no regret—no fear
    radiators, lacklove, torture even toothache in the end—

Though while it comes it is a lion that eats the soul—and the
    lamb, the soul, in us, alas, offering itself in sacrifice to
    change's fierce hunger—hair and teeth—and the roar
    of bonepain, skull bare, break rib, rot-skin, braintricked
    Implacability.

Ai! ai! we do worse! We are in a fix! And you're out, Death
    let you out, Death had the Mercy, you're done with your
    century, done with God, done with the path thru it—
    Done with yourself at last—Pure—Back to the Babe
    dark before your Father, before us all—before the
    world—

There, rest. No more suffering for you. I know where you've gone,
    it's good.

No more flowers in the summer fields of New York, no joy now,
    no more fear of Louis,

and no more of his sweetness and glasses, his high school decades,
    debts, loves, frightened telephone calls, conception beds,
    relatives, hands—

No more of sister Elanor,—she gone before you—we kept it
    secret—you killed her—or she killed herself to bear
    with you—an arthritic heart—But Death's killed you
    both—No matter—

Nor your memory of your mother, 1915 tears in silent movies
    weeks and weeks forgetting, agrieve watching Marie
    Dressler address humanity, Chaplin dance in youth,

or Boris Godounov, Chaliapin's at the Met, hailing his voice of
    a weeping Czar—by standing room with Elanor & Max
    —watching also the Capitalists take seats in Orchestra,
    white furs, diamonds,

with the YPSL's hitch-hiking thru Pennsylvania, in black baggy
    gym skirts pants, photograph of 4 girls holding each other
    round the waist, and laughing eye, too coy, virginal
    solitude of 1920

all girls grown old, or dead, now, and that long hair in the
    grave—lucky to have husbands later

You made it—I came too—Eugene my brother before (still
    grieving now and will gream on to his last stiff hand, as
    he goes thru his cancer—or kill—later perhaps—soon
    he will think—)

And it's the last moment I remember, which I see them all,
    thru myself, now—tho not you

I didn't foresee what you felt—what more hideous gape of
    bad mouth came first—to you—and were you prepared?

To go where? In that Dark—that—in that God? a radiance?
    A Lord in the Void? Like an eye in the black cloud in a
    dream? Adonoi at last, with you?

Beyond my remembrance! Incapable to guess! Not merely the
    yellow skull in the grave, or a box of worm dust, and
    a stained ribbon—Deathshead with Halo? can you
    believe it?

Is it only the sun that shines once for the mind, only the flash
    of existence, than none ever was?

Nothing beyond what we have—what you had—that so pitiful
    —yet Triumph,

to have been here, and changed, like a tree, broken, or flower—
    fed to the ground—but mad, with its petals, colored,
    thinking Great Universe, shaken, cut in the head, leaf
    stript, hid in an egg crate hospital, cloth wrapped, sore
    —freaked in the moon brain, Naughtless.

No flower like that flower, which knew itself in the garden, and
    fought the knife—lost

Cut down by an idiot Snowman's icy—even in the Spring—
  strange ghost thought—some Death—Sharp icicle in
  his hand crowned with old roses—a dog for his eyes
  —cock of a sweatshop—heart of electric irons.
All the accumulations of life, that wear us out—clocks, bodies,
  consciousness, shoes, breasts—begotten sons—your Com-
  munism—'Paranoia' into hospitals.
You once kicked Elanor in the leg, she died of heart failure
  later. You of stroke. Asleep? within a year, the two of
  you, sisters in death. Is Elanor happy?
Max grieves alive in an office on Lower Broadway, lone large
  mustache over midnight Accountings, not sure. His life
  passes—as he sees—and what does he doubt now?
  Still dream of making money, or that might have made
  money, hired nurse, had children, found even your
  Immortality, Naomi?
I'll see him soon. Now I've got to cut through—to talk to you
  —as I didn't when you had a mouth.
Forever. And we're bound for that, Forever—like Emily
  Dickinson's horses—headed to the End.
They know the way—These Steeds—run faster than we think
  —it's our own life they cross—and take with them.

  Magnificent, mourned no more, marred of heart, mind
behind, married dreamed, mortal changed—Ass and face done
with murder.

  In the world, given, flower maddened, made no Utopia,
shut under pine, aimed in Earth, balmed in Lone, Jehovah,
accept.

  Nameless, One Faced, Forever beyond me, beginningless,
endless, Father in death. Tho I am not there for this Prophecy,
I am unmarried, I'm hymnless, I'm Heavenless, headless in

blisshood I would still adore

Thee, Heaven, after Death, only One blessed in Nothingness, not light or darkness, Dayless Eternity—

Take this, this Psalm, from me, burst from my hand in a day, some of my Time, now given to Nothing—to praise Thee —But Death

This is the end, the redemption from Wilderness, way for the Wonderer, House sought for All, black handkerchief washed clean by weeping—page beyond Psalm—Last change of mine and Naomi—to God's perfect Darkness—Death, stay thy phantoms!

II

Over   and   over—refrain—of   the   Hospitals—still haven't written your history—leave it abstract—a few images
run thru the mind—like the saxophone chorus of houses and years—remembrance of electrical shocks.

By long nites as a child in Paterson apartment, watching over your nervousness—you were fat—your next move—

By that afternoon I stayed home from school to take care of you—once and for all—when I vowed forever that once man disagreed with my opinion of the cosmos, I was lost—

By my later burden—vow to illuminate mankind—this is release of particulars—(mad as you)—(sanity a trick of agreement)—

But you stared out the window on the Broadway Church corner, and spied a mystical assassin from Newark,

So phoned the Doctor—'OK go way for a rest'—so I put on my coat and walked you downstreet—On the way a grammarschool boy screamed, unaccountably—'Where you goin Lady to Death'? I shuddered—

and you covered your nose with motheaten fur collar, gas mask against poison sneaked into downtown atmosphere, sprayed by Grandma—

And was the driver of the cheesebox Public Service bus a member of the gang? You shuddered at his face, I could hardly get you on—to New York, very Times Square, to grab another Greyhound—

where we hung around 2 hours fighting invisible bugs and jewish sickness—breeze poisoned by Roosevelt—

out to get you—and me tagging along, hoping it would end in a quiet room in a victorian house by a lake.

Ride 3 hours thru tunnels past all American industry, Bayonne preparing for World War II, tanks, gas fields, soda

factories, diners, locomotive roundhouse fortress—into piney
woods New Jersey Indians—calm towns—long roads thru
sandy tree fields—

Bridges by deerless creeks, old wampum loading the
streambed—down there a tomahawk or Pocahontas bone—and
a million old ladies voting for Roosevelt in brown small houses,
roads off the Madness highway—

perhaps a hawk in a tree, or a hermit looking for an
owl-filled branch—

All the time arguing—afraid of strangers in the forward
double seat, snoring regardless—what busride they snore on
now?

'Allen, you don't understand—it's—ever since those
3 big sticks up my back—they did something to me in Hospital,
they poisoned me, they want to see me dead—3 big sticks, 3 big
sticks—

'The Bitch! Old Grandma! Last week I saw her, dressed
in pants like an old man, with a sack on her back, climbing up
the brick side of the apartment

'On the fire escape, with poison germs, to throw on me—
at night—maybe Louis is helping her—he's under her power—

'I'm your mother, take me to Lakewood' (near where
Graf Zeppelin had crashed before, all Hitler in Explosion)
'where I can hide.'

We got there—Dr. Whatzis rest home—she hid behind
a closet—demanded a blood transfusion.

We were kicked out—tramping with Valise to unknown
shady lawn houses—dusk, pine trees after dark—long dead
street filled with crickets and poison ivy—

I shut her up by now—big house REST HOME
ROOMS—gave the landlady her money for the week—carried
up the iron valise—sat on bed waiting to escape—

Neat room in attic with friendly bedcover—lace curtains

—spinning wheel rug—Stained wallpaper old as Naomi. We were home.

I left on the next bus to New York—lay my head back in the last seat, depressed—the worst yet to come?—abandoning her, rode in torpor—I was only 12.

Would she hide in her room and come out cheerful for breakfast? Or lock her door and stare thru the window for side-street spies? Listen at keyholes for Hitlerian invisible gas? Dream in a chair—or mock me, by—in front of a mirror, alone?

12 riding the bus at nite thru New Jersey, have left Naomi to Parcae in Lakewood's haunted house—left to my own fate bus—sunk in a seat—all violins broken—my heart sore in my ribs—mind was empty—Would she were safe in her coffin—

Or back at Normal School in Newark, studying up on America in a black skirt—winter on the street without lunch —a penny a pickle—home at night to take care of Elanor in the bedroom—

First nervous breakdown was 1919—she stayed home from school and lay in a dark room for three weeks—something bad—never said what—every noise hurt—dreams of the creaks of Wall Street—

Before the gray Depression went upstate New York— recovered—Lou took photo of her sitting crossleg on the grass —her long hair wound with flowers—smiling—playing lullabies on mandolin—poison ivy smoke in left-wing summer camps and me in infancy saw trees—

or back teaching school, laughing with idiots, the backward classes—her Russian specialty—morons with dreamy lips, great eyes, thin feet & sicky fingers, swaybacked, rachitic—

great heads pendulous over Alice in Wonderland, a black-
board full of C A T.

Naomi reading patiently, story out of a Communist fairy
book—Tale of the Sudden Sweetness of The Dictator—For-
giveness of Warlocks—Armies Kissing—

Deathsheads Around the Green Table—The King & the
Workers—Paterson Press printed them up in the 30's till she
went mad, or they folded, both.

O Paterson! I got home late that nite. Louis was
worried. How could I be so—didn't I think? I shouldn't have
left her. Mad in Lakewood. Call the Doctor. Phone the home
in the pines. Too late.

Went to bed exhausted, wanting to leave the world
(probably that year newly in love with R—my high school
mind hero, jewish boy who came a doctor later—then silent
neat kid—

I later laying down life for him, moved to Manhattan—
followed him to college—Prayed on ferry to help mankind if
admitted—vowed, the day I journeyed to Entrance Exam—
by being honest revolutionary labor lawyer—would train
for that—inspired by Sacco Vanzetti, Norman Thomas, Debs,
Altgeld, Sandburg, Poe—Little Blue Books. I wanted to be
President, or Senator.

ignorant woe—later dreams of kneeling by R's shocked
knees declaring my love of 1941—What sweetness he'd have
shown me, tho, that I'd wished him & despaired—first love—
a crush—

Later a mortal avalanche, whole mountains of homosexu-
ality, Matterhorns of cock, Grand Canyons of asshole—weight
on my melancholy head—

meanwhile I walked on Broadway imagining Infinity like
a rubber ball without space beyond—what's outside?—coming

home to Graham Avenue still melancholy passing the lone green hedges across the street, dreaming after the movies—)

The telephone rang at 2AM—Emergency—she'd gone mad—Naomi hiding under the bed screaming bugs of Mussolini —Help! Louis! Buba! Fascists! Death!—the landlady frightened—old fag attendant screaming back at her—

Terror, that woke the neighbors—old ladies on the second floor recovering from menopause—all those rags between thighs, clean sheets, sorry over lost babies—husbands ashen— children sneering at Yale, or putting oil in hair at CCNY—or trembling in Montclair State Teachers College like Eugene—

Her big leg crouched to her breast, hand outstretched Keep Away, wool dress on her thighs, fur coat dragged under the bed—she barricaded herself under bedspring with suitcases.

Louis in pajamas listening to phone, frightened—do now?—Who could know?—my fault, delivering her to solitude?—sitting in the dark room on the sofa, trembling, to figure out—

He took the morning train to Lakewood, Naomi still under bed—thought he brought poison Cops—Naomi screaming— Louis what happened to your heart then? Have you been killed by Naomi's ecstasy?

Dragged her out, around the corner, a cab, forced her in with valise, but the driver left them off at drugstore. Bus stop, two hours' wait.

I lay in bed nervous in the 4-room apartment, the big bed in living room, next to Louis' desk—shaking—he came home that nite, late, told me what happened.

Naomi at the prescription counter defending herself from the enemy—racks of children's books, douche bags, aspirins, pots, blood—'Don't come near me—murderers! Keep away! Promise not to kill me!'

Louis in horror at the soda fountain with Lakewood girlscouts—coke addicts—nurses—busmen hung on schedule —Police from country precinct, dumbed—and a priest dreaming of pigs on an ancient cliff?

Smelling the air—Louis pointing to emptiness?— Customers vomiting their cokes—or staring—Louis humiliated —Naomi triumphant—The Announcement of the Plot. Bus arrives, the drivers won't have them on trip to New York.

Phonecalls to Dr. Whatzis, 'She needs a rest,' The mental hospital—State Greystone Doctors—'Bring her here, Mr. Ginsberg.'

Naomi, Naomi—sweating, bulge-eyed, fat, the dress unbuttoned at one side—hair over brow, her stocking hanging evilly on her legs—screaming for a blood transfusion—one righteous hand upraised—a shoe in it—barefoot in the Pharmacy—

The enemies approach—what poisons? Tape recorders? FBI? Zhdanov hiding behind the counter? Trotsky mixing rat bacteria in the back of the store? Uncle Sam in Newark, plotting deathly perfumes in the Negro district? Uncle Ephraim, drunk with murder in the politician's bar, scheming of Hague? Aunt Rose passing water thru the needles of the Spanish Civil War?

till the hired $35 ambulance came from Red Bank— —Grabbed her arms—strapped her on the stretcher—moaning, poisoned by imaginaries, vomiting chemicals thru Jersey, begging mercy from Essex County to Morristown—

And back to Greystone where she lay three years—that was the last breakthrough, delivered her to Madhouse again—

On what wards—I walked there later, oft—old catatonic ladies, gray as cloud or ash or walls—sit crooning over floorspace—Chairs—and the wrinkled hags acreep, accusing

—begging my 13-year-old mercy—

'Take me home'—I went alone sometimes looking for the lost Naomi, taking Shock—and I'd say, 'No, you're crazy Mama,—Trust the Drs.'—

And Eugene, my brother, her elder son, away studying Law in a furnished room in Newark—

came Paterson-ward next day—and he sat on the broken-down couch in the living room—'We had to send her back to Greystone'—

—his face perplexed, so young, then eyes with tears—then crept weeping all over his face—'What for?' wail vibrating in his cheekbones, eyes closed up, high voice—Eugene's face of pain.

Him faraway, escaped to an Elevator in the Newark Library, his bottle daily milk on windowsill of $5 week furn room downtown at trolley tracks—

He worked 8 hrs. a day for $20/wk—thru Law School years—stayed by himself innocent near negro whorehouses.

Unlaid, poor virgin—writing poems about Ideals and politics letters to the editor Pat Eve News—(we both wrote, denouncing Senator Borah and Isolationists—and felt mysterious toward Paterson City Hall—

I sneaked inside it once—local Moloch tower with phallus spire & cap o' ornament, strange gothic Poetry that stood on Market Street—replica Lyons' Hotel de Ville—

wings, balcony & scrollwork portals, gateway to the giant city clock, secret map room full of Hawthorne—dark Debs in the Board of Tax—Rembrandt smoking in the gloom—

Silent polished desks in the great committee room—Aldermen? Bd of Finance? Mosca the hairdresser aplot—Crapp the gangster issuing orders from the john—The madmen struggling over Zone, Fire, Cops & Backroom Metaphysics—we're all dead—outside by the bus-stop Eugene stared thru child-hood—

where the Evangelist preached madly for 3 decades, hard-haired, cracked & true to his mean Bible—chalked Prepare to Meet Thy God on civic pave—

or God is Love on the railroad overpass concrete—he raved like I would rave, the lone Evangelist—Death on City Hall—)

But Gene, young, been Montclair Teachers College 4 years—taught half year & quit to go ahead in life—afraid of Discipline Problems—dark sex Italian students, raw girls getting laid, no English, sonnets disregarded—and he did not know much—just that he lost—

so broke his life in two and paid for Law—read huge blue hooks and rode the ancient elevator 13 miles away in Newark & studied up hard for the future

just found the Scream of Naomi on his failure doorstep, for the final time, Naomi gone, us lonely—home—him sitting there—

Then have some chicken soup, Eugene. The man of Evangel wails in front of City Hall. And this year Lou has poetic loves of suburb middle-age—in secret—music from his 1937 book—Sincere—he longs for beauty—

No love since Naomi screamed—since 1923?—now lost in Greystone ward—new shock for her—Electricity, following the 40 Insulin.

And Metrasol had made her fat.

So that a few years later she came home again—we'd much advanced and planned—I waited for that day—my Mother again to cook &—play the piano sing at mandolin —Lung Stew, & Stenka Razin, & the communist line on the war with Finland—and Louis in debt—suspected to be poisoned money—mysterious capitalisms

—& walked down the long front hall & looked at the furniture. She never remembered it all. Some amnesia. Examined the doilies—and the dining room set was sold—

the Mahogany table—20 years love—gone to the junk man—we still had the piano—and the book of Poe—and the Mandolin, tho needed some string, dusty—

She went to the backroom to lay down in bed and ruminate, or nap, hide—I went in with her, not leave her by herself—lay in bed next to her—shades pulled, dusky, late afternoon—Louis in front room at desk, waiting—perhaps boiling chicken for supper—

'Don't be afraid of me because I'm just coming back home from the mental hospital—I'm your mother—'

Poor love, lost—a fear—I lay there—Said, 'I love you Naomi,'—stiff, next to her arm. I would have cried, was this the comfortless lone union?—Nervous, and she got up soon.

Was she ever satisfied? And—by herself sat on the new couch by the front windows, uneasy—cheek leaning on her hand—narrowing eye—at what fate that day—

Picking her tooth with her nail, lips formed an O, suspicion—thought's old worn vagina—absent sideglance of eye—some evil debt written in the wall, unpaid—& the aged breasts of Newark come near—

May have heard radio gossip thru the wires in her head, controlled by 3 big sticks left in her back by gangsters in amnesia, thru the hospital—caused pain between her shoulders—

Into her head—Roosevelt should know her case, she told me—Afraid to kill her, now, that the government knew their names—traced back to Hitler—wanted to leave Louis' house forever.

One night, sudden attack—her noise in the bathroom—like croaking up her soul—convulsions and red vomit coming out of her mouth—diarrhea water exploding from her behind—on all fours in front of the toilet—urine running between her legs—left retching on the tile floor smeared with her black feces—unfainted—

At forty, varicosed, nude, fat, doomed, hiding outside the apartment door near the elevator calling Police, yelling for her girlfriend Rose to help—

Once locked herself in with razor or iodine—could hear her cough in tears at sink—Lou broke through glass green-painted door, we pulled her out to the bedroom.

Then quiet for months that winter—walks, alone, nearby on Broadway, read Daily Worker—Broke her arm, fell on icy street—

Began to scheme escape from cosmic financial murder plots—later she ran away to the Bronx to her sister Elanor. And there's another saga of late Naomi in New York.

Or thru Elanor or the Workman's Circle, where she worked, addressing envelopes, she made out—went shopping for Campbell's tomato soup—saved money Louis mailed her—

Later she found a boyfriend, and he was a doctor—Dr. Isaac worked for National Maritime Union—now Italian bald and pudgy old doll—who was himself an orphan—but they kicked him out—Old cruelties—

Sloppier, sat around on bed or chair, in corset dreaming to herself—'I'm hot—I'm getting fat—I used to have such a beautiful figure before I went to the hospital—You should have seen me in Woodbine—' This in a furnished room around the NMU hall, 1943.

Looking at naked baby pictures in the magazine—baby

powder advertisements, strained lamb carrots — 'I will think nothing but beautiful thoughts.'

Revolving her head round and round on her neck at window light in summertime, in hypnotize, in doven-dream recall —

'I touch his cheek, I touch his cheek, he touches my lips with his hand, I think beautiful thoughts, the baby has a beautiful hand.' —

Or a No-shake of her body, disgust — some thought of Buchenwald — some insulin passes thru her head — a grimace nerve shudder at Involuntary (as shudder when I piss) — bad chemical in her cortex — 'No don't think of that. He's a rat.'

Naomi: 'And when we die we become an onion, a cabbage, a carrot, or a squash, a vegetable.' I come downtown from Columbia and agree. She reads the Bible, thinks beautiful thoughts all day.

'Yesterday I saw God. What did he look like? Well, in the afternoon I climbed up a ladder — he has a cheap cabin in the country, like Monroe, NY the chicken farms in the wood. He was a lonely old man with a white beard.

'I cooked supper for him. I made him a nice supper — lentil soup, vegetables, bread & butter — miltz — he sat down at the table and ate, he was sad.

'I told him, Look at all those fightings and killings down there, What's the matter? Why don't you put a stop to it?

'I try, he said — That's all he could do, he looked tired. He's a bachelor so long, and he likes lentil soup.'

Serving me meanwhile, a plate of cold fish — chopped raw cabbage dript with tapwater — smelly tomatoes — week-old health food — grated beets & carrots with leaky juice, warm — more and more disconsolate food — I can't eat it for nausea sometimes — the Charity of her hands stinking with Manhattan, madness, desire to please me, cold undercooked fish—pale red near the bones. Her smells—and oft naked in the room, so that I stare ahead, or turn a book ignoring her.

One time I thought she was trying to make me come lay her—flirting to herself at sink—lay back on huge bed that filled most of the room, dress up round her hips, big slash of 'hair, scars of operations, pancreas, belly wounds, abortions, appendix, stitching of incisions pulling down in the fat like hideous thick zippers—ragged long lips between her legs— What, even, smell of asshole? I was cold—later revolted a little, not much—seemed perhaps a good idea to try—know the Monster of the Beginning Womb—Perhaps—that way. Would she care? She needs a lover.

Yisborach, v'yistabach, v'yispoar, v'yisroman, v'yisnaseh, v'yishador, v'yishalleh, v'yishallol, sh'rneh d'kudsho, b'rich hu. And Louis reestablishing himself in Paterson grimy apartment in negro district—living in dark rooms—but found himself a girl he later married, falling in love again—tho sere & shy—hurt with 20 years Naomi's mad idealism.

Once I came home, after longtime in NY, he's lonely— sitting in the bedroom, he at desk chair turned round to face me —weeps, tears in red eyes under his glasses—

That we'd left him—Gene gone strangely into army— she out on her own in NY, almost childish in her furnished room. So Louis walked downtown to postoffice to get mail, taught in highschool—stayed at poetry desk, forlorn—ate grief at Bickford's all these years—are gone.

Eugene got out of the Army, came home changed and lone—cut off his nose in jewish operation—for years stopped girls on Broadway for cups of coffee to get laid—Went to NYU, serious there, to finish Law.—

And Gene lived with her, ate naked fishcakes, cheap,

while she got crazier—He got thin, or felt helpless, Naomi
striking 1920 poses at the moon, half-naked in the next bed.

bit his nails and studied—was the weird nurse-son—
Next year he moved to a room near Columbia—though she
wanted to live with her children—

'Listen to your mother's plea, I beg you'—Louis still
sending her checks—I was in bughouse that year 8 months—
my own visions unmentioned in this here Lament—

But then went half mad—Hitler in her room, she saw
his mustache in the sink—afraid of Dr. Isaac now, suspecting
that he was in on the Newark plot—went up to Bronx to live
near Elanor's Rheumatic Heart—

And Uncle Max never got up before noon, tho Naomi at
6 AM was listening to the radio for spies—or searching the
windowsill,

for in the empty lot downstairs, an old man creeps with
his bag stuffing packages of garbage in his hanging black
overcoat.

Max's sister Edie works—17 years bookeeper at Gimbels
—lived downstairs in apartment house, divorced—so Edie took
in Naomi on Rochambeau Ave—

Woodlawn Cemetery across the street, vast dale of graves
where Poe once—Last stop on Bronx subway—lots of com-
munists in that area.

Who enrolled for painting classes at night in Bronx Adult
High School—walked alone under Van Cortlandt Elevated
line to class—paints Naomiisms—

Humans sitting on the grass in some Camp No-Worry
summers yore—saints with droopy faces and long-ill-fitting
pants, from hospital—

Brides in front of Lower East Side with short grooms—

lost El trains running over the Babylonian apartment rooftops in the Bronx—

Sad paintings—but she expressed herself. Her mandolin gone, all strings broke in her head, she tried. Toward Beauty? or some old life Message?

But started kicking Elanor, and Elanor had heart trouble —came upstairs and asked her about Spydom for hours,— Elanor frazzled. Max away at office, accounting for cigar stores till at night.

'I am a great woman—am truly a beautiful soul—and because of that they (Hitler, Grandma, Hearst, the Capitalists, Franco, Daily News, the 20's, Mussolini, the living dead) want to shut me up—Buba's the head of a spider network—'

Kicking the girls, Edie & Elanor—Woke Edie at midnite to tell her she was a spy and Elanor a rat. Edie worked all day and couldn't take it—She was organizing the union.—And Elanor began dying, upstairs in bed.

The relatives call me up, she's getting worse—I was the only one left—Went on the subway with Eugene to see her, ate stale fish—

'My sister whispers in the radio—Louis must be in the apartment—his mother tells him what to say—LIARS!—I cooked for my two children—I played the mandolin—'

Last night the nightingale woke me/ Last night when all was still/ it sang in the golden moonlight/ from on the wintry hill. She did.

I pushed her against the door and shouted 'DON'T KICK ELANOR!'—she stared at me—Contempt—die— disbelief her sons are so naive, so dumb—' Elanor is the worst spy! She's taking orders!'

'—No wires in the room!'—I'm yelling at her—last ditch, Eugene listening on the bed—what can he do to escape

that fatal Mama—You've been away from Louis years already
—Grandma's too old to walk—'

We're all alive at once then—even me & Gene & Naomi
in one mythological Cousinesque room—screaming at each
other in the Forever—I in Columbia jacket, she half undressed.
I banging against her head which saw Radios, Sticks,
Hitlers—the gamut of Hallucinations—for real—her own
universe—no road that goes elsewhere—to my own—No
America, not even a world—

That you go as all men, as Van Gogh, as mad Hannah,
all the same—to the last doom—Thunder, Spirits, Lightning!
I've seen your grave! O strange Naomi! My own—
cracked grave! Shema Y'Israel—I am Svul Avrum—you—
in death?

Your last night in the darkness of the Bronx—I phone-
called—thru hospital to secret police.

That came, when you and I were alone, shrieking at
Elanor in my ear—who breathed hard in her own bed, got
thin—

Nor Will forget, the doorknock, at your fright of spies,—
Law advancing, on my honor—Eternity entering the room—
you running to the bathroom undressed, hiding in protest from
the last heroic fate—

staring at my eyes, betrayed—the final cops of madness
rescuing me—from your foot against the broken heart of
Elanor,

your voice at Edie weary of Gimbels coming home to
broken radio—and Louis needing a poor divorce, he wants to
get married soon—Eugene dreaming, hiding at 125 St., suing
negroes for money on crud furniture, defending black girls—

Protests from the bathroom—Said you were sane—

dressing in a cotton robe, your shoes, then new, your purse and newspaper clippings—no—your honesty—

as you vainly made your lips more real with lipstick, looking in the mirror to see if the Insanity was Me or a earful of police.

or Grandma spying at 78—Your vision—Her climbing over the walls of the cemetery with political kidnapper's bag— or what you saw on the walls of the Bronx, in pink nightgown at midnight, staring out the window on the empty lot—

Ah Rochambeau Ave—Playground of Phantoms—last apartment in the Bronx for spies—last home for Elanor or Naomi, here these communist sisters lost their revolution—

'All right—put on your coat Mrs.—let's go—We have the wagon downstairs—you want to come with her to the station?'

The ride then—held Naomi's hand, and held her head to my breast, I'm taller—kissed her and said I did it for the best—Elanor sick—and Max with heart condition—Needs—

To me—'Why did you do this?'—'Yes Mrs., your son will have to leave you in an hour'—The Ambulance

came in a few hours—drove off at 4 AM to some Bellevue in the night downtown—gone to the hospital forever. I saw her led away—she waved, tears in her eyes.

Two years, after a trip to Mexico—bleak in the flat plain near Brentwood, scrub brush and grass around the unused RR train track to the crazyhouse—

new brick 20 story central building—lost on the vast lawns of madtown on Long Island—huge cities of the moon.

Asylum spreads out giant wings above the path to a minute black hole—the door—entrance thru crotch—

I went in—smelt funny—the halls again—up elevator —to a glass door on a Woman's Ward—to Naomi—Two nurses buxom white—They led her out, Naomi stared—and I gaspt—She'd had a stroke—

Too thin, shrunk on her bones—age come to Naomi— now broken into white hair—loose dress on her skeleton— face sunk, old! withered—cheek of crone—

One hand stiff—heaviness of forties & menopause re- duced by one heart stroke, lame now—wrinkles—a scar on her head, the lobotomy—ruin, the hand dipping downwards to death—

O Russian faced, woman on the grass, your long black hair is crowned with flowers, the mandolin is on your knees—

Communist beauty, sit here married in the summer among daisies, promised happiness at hand—

holy mother, now you smile on your love, your world is born anew, children run naked in the field spotted with dandelions,

they eat in the plum tree grove at the end of the meadow and find a cabin where a white-haired negro teaches the mystery of his rainbarrel—

blessed daughter come to America, I long to hear your voice again, remembering your mother's music, in the Song of the Natural Front—

O glorious muse that bore me from the womb, gave suck first mystic life & taught me talk and music, from whose pained head I first took Vision—

Tortured and beaten in the skull What mad hallucina- tions of the damned that drive me out of my own skull to seek Eternity till I find Peace for Thee, O Poetry—and for all humankind call on the Origin

Death which is the mother of the universe!—Now wear
your nakedness forever, white flowers in your hair, your marriage
sealed behind the sky—no revolution might destroy that
maidenhood—

O beautiful Garbo of my Karma—all photographs from
1920 in Camp Nicht-Gedeiget here unchanged—with all the
teachers from Newark—Nor Elanor be gone, nor Max await
his specter nor Louis retire from this High School—

Back! You! Naomi! Skull on you! Gaunt immortality
and revolution come—small broken woman—the ashen indoor
eyes of hospitals, ward greyness on skin—

'Are you a spy?' I sat at the sour table, eyes filling with
tears—'Who are you? Did Louis send you?—The wires—'
in her hair, as she beat on her head—'I'm not a bad
girl don't murder me!—I hear the ceiling—I raised two
children—'

Two years since I'd been there—I started to cry—She
stared—nurse broke up the meeting a moment—I went into
the bathroom to hide, against the toilet white walls

'The Horror' I weeping—to see her again—'The
Horror'—as if she were dead thru funeral rot in—'The
Horror!'

I came back she yelled more—they led her away—
'You're not Allen—' I watched her face—but she passed by
me, not looking—

Opened the door to the ward,—she went thru without
a glance back, quiet suddenly—I stared out—she looked old
—the verge of the grave—'All the Horror!'

Another year, I left NY—on West Coast in Berkeley
cottage dreamed of her soul—that, thru life, in what form it

stood in that body, ashen or manic, gone beyond joy—

near its death—with eyes—was my own love in its form, the Naomi, my mother on earth still—sent her long letter —& wrote hymns to the mad—Work of the merciful Lord of Poetry.

that causes the broken grass to be green, or the rock to break in grass—or the Sun to be constant to earth—Sun of all sunflowers and days on bright iron bridges—what shines on old hospitals—as on my yard—

Returning from San Francisco one night, Orlovsky in my room—Whalen in his peaceful chair—a telegram from Gene, Naomi dead—

Outside I bent my head to the ground under the bushes near the garage—knew she was better—

at last—not left to look on Earth alone—2 years of solitude—no one, at age nearing 60—old woman of skulls— once long-tressed Naomi of Bible—

or Ruth who wept in America—Rebecca aged in Newark David remembering his Harp, now lawyer at Yale

or Svul Avrum—Israel Abraham—myself—to sing in the wilderness toward God—O Elohim!—so to the end—2 days after her death I got her letter—

Strange Prophecies anew! She wrote—'The key is in the window, the key is in the sunlight at the window—I have the key—Get married Allen don't take drugs—the key is in the bars, in the sunlight in the window.

Love,

your mother'

which is Naomi—

HYMMNN

In the world which He has created according to his will Blessed
  Praised

Magnified Lauded Exalted the Name of the Holy One Blessed
  is He!

In the house in Newark Blessed is He! In the madhouse Blessed
  is He! In the house of Death Blessed is He!

Blessed be He in homosexuality! Blessed be He in Paranoia!
  Blessed be He in the city! Blessed be He in the Book!

Blessed be He who dwells in the shadow! Blessed be He!
  Blessed he He!

Blessed be you Naomi in tears! Blessed be you Naomi in fears!
  Blessed Blessed Blessed in sickness!

Blessed be you Naomi in Hospitals! Blessed be you Naomi in
  solitude! Blest be your triumph! Blest be your bars!
  Blest be your last years' loneliness!

Blest be your failure! Blest be your stroke! Blest be the close
  of your eye! Blest be the gaunt of your cheek! Blest be
  your withered thighs!

Blessed be Thee Naomi in Death! Blessed be Death! Blessed
  be Death!

Blessed be He Who leads all sorrow to Heaven! Blessed be
  He in the end I

Blessed be He who builds Heaven in Darkness! Blessed Blessed
  Blessed be He! Blessed be He! Blessed be Death on
  us All!

III

Only to have not forgotten the beginning in which she drank
cheap sodas in the morgues of Newark,

only to have seen her weeping on grey tables in long wards of
her universe

only to have known the weird ideas of Hitler at the door, the
wires in her head, the three big sticks

rammed down her back, the voices in the ceiling shrieking out
her ugly early lays for 30 years,

only to have seen the time-jumps, memory lapse, the crash of
wars, the roar and silence of a vast electric shock,

only to have seen her painting crude pictures of Elevateds
running over the rooftops of the Bronx

her brothers dead in Riverside or Russia, her lone in Long
Island writing a last letter—and her image in the sun-
light at the window

'The key is in the sunlight at the window in the bars the key
is in the sunlight,'

only to have come to that dark night on iron bed by stroke when
the sun gone down on Long Island

and the vast Atlantic roars outside the great call of Being to
its own

to come back out of the Nightmare divided creation—with
her head lain on a pillow of the hospital to die

—in one last glimpse—all Earth one everlasting Light in the
familiar blackout—no tears for this vision—

But that the key should be left behind—at the window—the
key in the sunlight—to the living—that can take

that slice of light in hand—and turn the door—and look
back see

Creation glistening backwards to the same grave, size of universe,

size of the tick of the hospital's clock on the archway over the
white door—

IV

O mother
what have I left out
O mother
what have I forgotten
O mother farewell
with a long black shoe
farewell
with Communist Party and a broken stocking
farewell
with six dark hairs on the wen of your breast
farewell
with your old dress and a long black beard around the vagina
farewell
with your sagging belly
with your fear of Hitler
with your mouth of bad short stories
with your fingers of rotten mandolins
with your arms of fat Paterson porches
with your belly of strikes and smokestacks
with your chin of Trotsky and the Spanish War
with your voice singing for the decaying overbroken workers
with your nose of bad lay with your nose of the smell of the
        pickles of Newark
with your eyes
with your eyes of Russia
with your eyes of no money
with your eyes of false China
with your eyes of Aunt Elanor
with your eyes of starving India
with your eyes pissing in the park

with your eyes of America taking a fall
with your eyes of your failure at the piano
with your eyes of your relatives in California
with your eyes of Ma Rainey dying in an ambulance
with your eyes of Czechoslovakia attacked by robots
with your eyes going to painting class at night in the Bronx
with your eyes of the killer Grandma you see on the horizon
    from the Fire-Escape
with your eyes running naked out of the apartment screaming
    into the hall
with your eyes being led away by policemen to an ambulance
with your eyes strapped down on the operating table
with your eyes with the pancreas removed
with your eyes of appendix operation
with your eyes of abortion
with your eyes of ovaries removed
with your eyes of shock
with your eyes of lobotomy
with your eyes of divorce
with your eyes of stroke
with your eyes alone
with your eyes
with your eyes
with your Death full of Flowers

V

Caw caw caw crows shriek in the white sun over grave stones
in Long Island
Lord Lord Lord Naomi underneath this grass my halflife and
my own as hers
caw caw my eye be buried in the same Ground where I stand
in Angel
Lord Lord great Eye that stares on All and moves in a black
cloud
caw caw strange cry of Beings flung up into sky over the waving
trees
Lord Lord O Grinder of giant Beyonds my voice in a boundless
field in Sheol
Caw caw the call of Time rent out of foot and wing an instant
in the universe
Lord Lord an echo in the sky the wind through ragged leaves
the roar of memory
caw caw all years my birth a dream caw caw New York the bus
the broken shoe the vast highschool caw caw all Visions
of the Lord
Lord Lord Lord caw caw caw Lord Lord Lord caw caw caw
Lord

NY 1959

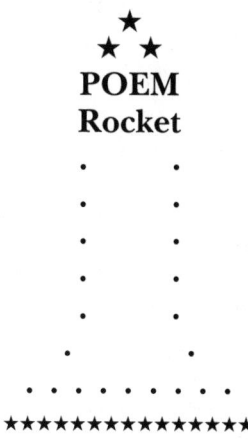

**POEM
Rocket**

'Be a Star-screwer!'—Gregory Corso

Old moon my eyes are new moon with human footprint
no longer Romeo Sadface in drunken river Loony Pierre eye-
    brow, goof moon
O possible moon in Heaven we get to first of ageless constella-
    tions of names
as God is possible as All is possible so we'll reach another life.

Moon politicians earth weeping and warring in eternity
tho not one star disturbed by screaming madmen from
    Hollywood
oil tycoons from Romania making secret deals with flabby green
    Plutonians—
slave camps on Saturn Cuban revolutions on Mars?
Old life and new side by side, will Catholic church find Christ
    on Jupiter

Mohammed rave in Uranus will Buddha be acceptable on the
    stolid planets
or will we find Zoroastrian temples flowering on Neptune?
What monstrous new ecclesiastical design on the entire universe
    unfolds in the dying Pope's brain?
Scientist alone is true poet he gives us the moon
he promises the stars he'll make us a new universe if it comes
    to that
O Einstein I should have sent you my flaming mss.
O Einstein I should have pilgrimaged to your white hair!

O fellow travelers I write you a poem in Amsterdam in the
    Cosmos
where Spinoza ground his magic lenses long ago
I write you a poem long ago
already my feet are washed in death
Here I am naked without identity
with no more body than the fine black tracery of pen mark on
    soft paper
as star talks to star multiple beams of sunlight all the same
    myriad thought
in one fold of the universe where Whitman was
and Blake and Shelley saw Milton dwelling as in a starry temple
    brooding in his blindness seeing all—
Now at last I can speak to you beloved brothers of an unknown
    moon
real Yous squatting in whatever form amidst Platonic Vapors of
    Eternity
I am another Star.
Will you eat my poems or read them
or gaze with aluminum blind plates on sunless pages?
do you dream or translate & accept data with indifferent

droopings of antennae?

do I make sense to your flowery green receptor eyesockets? Do you have visions of God?

Which way will the sunflower turn surrounded by millions of suns?

This is my rocket my personal rocket I send up my message Beyond

Someone to hear me there

My immortality

without steel or cobalt basalt or diamond gold or mercurial fire

without passports filing cabinets bits of paper warheads

without myself finally

pure thought

message all and everywhere the same

I send up my rocket to land on whatever planet awaits it

preferably religious sweet planets no money

fourth dimensional planets where Death shows movies

plants speak (courteously) of ancient physics and poetry itself is manufactured by the trees

the final Planet where the Great Brain of the Universe sits waiting for a poem to land in His golden pocket

joining the other notes mash-notes love-sighs complaints-musical shrieks of despair and the million unutterable thoughts of frogs

I send you my rocket of amazing chemical

more than my hair my sperm or the cells of my body

the speeding thought that flies upward with my desire as instantaneous as the universe and faster than light

and leave all other questions unfinished for the moment to turn back to sleep in my dark bed on earth.

Amsterdam 1958

EUROPE! EUROPE!

World world world
I sit in my room
imagine the future
sunlight falls on Paris
I am alone there is no
one whose love is perfect
man has been mad man's
love is not perfect I
have not wept enough
my breast will be heavy
till death the cities
are specters of cranks
of war the cities are
work & brick & iron &
smoke of the furnace of
selfhood makes tearless
eyes red in London but
no eye meets the sun

Flashed out of sky it
hits Lord Beaverbrook's
white modern solid
paper building leaned
in London's street to
bear last yellow beams
old ladies absently gaze
thru fog toward heaven
poor pots on windowsills
snake flowers to street
Trafalgar's fountains splash

on noon-warmed pigeons
Myself beaming in ecstatic
wilderness on St. Paul's dome
seeing the light on London
or here on a bed in Paris
sunglow through the high
window on plaster walls

Meek crowd underground
saints perish creeps
streetwomen meet lacklove
under gaslamp and neon
no woman in house loves
husband in flower unity
nor boy loves boy soft
fire in breast politics
electricity scares downtown
radio screams for money
police light on TV screens
laughs at dim lamps in
empty rooms tanks crash
thru bombshell no dream
of man's joy is made movie
think factory pushes junk
autos tin dreams of Eros
mind eats its flesh in
geekish starvation and no
man's fuck is holy for
man's work is most war

Bony China hungers brain
wash over power dam and
America hides mad meat
in refrigerator Britain
cooks Jerusalem too long
France eats oil and dead
salad arms & legs in Africa
loudmouth devours Arabia
negro and white warring
against the golden nuptial
Russia manufacture feeds
millions but no drunk can
dream Mayakovsky's suicide
rainbow over machinery
and back talk to the sun

I lie in bed in Europe
alone in old red under
wear symbolic of desire
for union with immortality
but man's love's not perfect
in February it rains
as once for Baudelaire
one hundred years ago
planes roar in the air
cars race thru streets
I know where they go
to death but that is OK
it is that death comes
before life that no man
has loved perfectly no one
gets bliss in time new

mankind is not born that
I weep for this antiquity
and herald the Millennium
for I saw the Atlantic sun
rayed down from a vast cloud
at Dover on the sea cliffs
tanker size of ant heaved
up on ocean under shining
cloud and seagull flying
thru sun light's endless
ladders streaming in Eternity
to ants in the myriad fields
of England to sun flowers
bent up to eat infinity's
minute gold dolphins leaping
thru Mediterranean rainbow
White smoke and steam in Andes
Asia's rivers glittering
blind poets deep in lone
Apollonic radiance on hillsides
littered with empty tombs

Paris 1958

TO LINDSAY

Vachel, the stars are out
dusk has fallen on the Colorado road
a car crawls slowly across the plain
in the dim light the radio blares its jazz
the heartbroken salesman lights another cigarette
In another city 27 years ago
I see your shadow on the wall
you're sitting in your suspenders on the bed
the shadow hand lifts up a Lysol bottle to your head
your shade falls over on the floor

Paris 1958

MESSAGE

Since we had changed
rogered spun worked
wept and pissed together
I wake up in the morning
with a dream in my eyes
but you are gone in NY
remembering me Good
I love you I love you
& your brothers are crazy
I accept their drunk cases
It's too long that I have been alone
it's too long that I've sat up in bed
without anyone to touch on the knee, man
or woman I don't care what anymore, I
want love I was born for I want you with me now
Ocean liners boiling over the Atlantic
Delicate steelwork of unfinished skyscrapers
Back end of the dirigible roaring over Lakehurst
Six women dancing together on a red stage naked
The leaves are green on all the trees in Paris now
I will be home in two months and look you in the eyes

1958

TO AUNT ROSE

Aunt Rose—now—might I see you
with your thin face and buck tooth smile and pain
        of rheumatism—and a long black heavy shoe
       for your bony left leg
   limping down the long hall in Newark on the running carpet
       past the black grand piano
        in the day room
           where the parties were
    and I sang Spanish loyalist songs
    in a high squeaky voice
       (hysterical) the committee listening
    while you limped around the room
      collected the money—
Aunt Honey, Uncle Sam, a stranger with a cloth arm
    in his pocket
      and huge young bald head
        of Abraham Lincoln Brigade

—your long sad face
      your tears of sexual frustration
        (what smothered sobs and bony hips
          under the pillows of Osborne Terrace)
   —the time I stood on the toilet seat naked
       and you powdered my thighs with Calomine
       against the poison ivy—my tender
        and shamed first black curled hairs
what were you thinking in secret heart then
    knowing me a man already—
and I an ignorant girl of family silence on the thin pedestal
    of my legs in the bathroom—Museum of Newark.

Aunt Rose

Hitler is dead, Hitler is in Eternity; Hitler is with
Tamburlane and. Emily Brontë

Though I see you walking still, a ghost on Osborne Terrace
down the long dark hall to the front door
limping a little with a pinched smile
in what must have been a silken
flower dress
welcoming my father, the Poet, on his visit to Newark
—see you arriving in the living room
dancing on your crippled leg
and clapping hands his book
had been accepted by Liveright

Hitler is dead and Liveright's gone out of business
The Attic of the Past and *Everlasting Minute* are out of print
Uncle Harry sold his last silk stocking
Claire quit interpretive dancing school
Buba sits a wrinkled monument in Old
Ladies Home blinking at new babies

last time I saw you was the hospital
pale skull protruding under ashen skin
blue veined unconscious girl
in an oxygen tent
the war in Spain has ended long ago
Aunt Rose

Paris 1958

AT APOLLINAIRE'S GRAVE

. . . voici le temps
Où l'on connaltra l'avenir
Sans mourir de connaissance

I

I visited Père Lachaise to look for the remains of Apollinaire
the day the U.S. President appeared in France for the grand
conference of heads of state
so let it be the airport at blue Orly a springtime clarity in the
air over Paris
Eisenhower winging in from his American graveyard
and over the froggy graves at Père Lachaise an illusory mist as
thick as marijuana smoke
Peter Orlovsky and I walked softly thru Père Lachaise we both
knew we would die
and so held temporary hands tenderly in a citylike miniature
eternity
roads and streetsigns rocks and hills and names on everybody's
house
looking for the lost address of a notable Frenchman of the Void
to pay our tender crime of homage to his helpless menhir
and lay my temporary American Howl on top of his silent
Calligramme
for him to read between the lines with Xray eyes of Poet
as he by miracle had read his own death lyric in the Seine
I hope some wild kidmonk lay his pamphlet on my grave for God
to read me on cold winter nights in heaven
already our hands have vanished from that place my hand writes
now in a room in Paris Git-Le-Coeur

Ah William what grit in the brain you had what's death
I walked all over the cemetery and still couldn't find your grave
what did you mean by that fantastic cranial bandage in your
poems
O solemn stinking deathshead what've you got to say nothing
and that's barely an answer

You can't drive autos into a sixfoot grave tho the universe is
mausoleum big enough for anything
the universe is a graveyard and I walk around alone in here
knowing that Apollinaire was on the same street 50 years ago
his madness is only around the corner and Genet is with us
stealing books
the West is at war again and whose lucid suicide will set it all
right
Guillaume Guillaume how I envy your fame your accomplish-
ment for American letters
your Zone with its long crazy line of bullshit about death
come out of the grave and talk thru the door of my mind
issue new series of images oceanic haikus blue taxicabs in Moscow
negro statues of Buddha
pray for me on the phonograph record of your former existence
with a long sad voice and strophes of deep sweet music sad and
scratchy as World War I
I've eaten the blue carrots you sent out of the grave and Van
Gogh's ear and maniac peyote of Artaud
and will walk down the streets of New York in the black cloak of
French poetry
improvising our conversation in Paris at Père Lachaise
and the future poem that takes its inspiration from the light
bleeding into your grave

II

Here in Paris I am your guest O friendly shade
the absent hand of Max Jacob
Picasso in youth bearing me a tube of Mediterranean
myself attending Rousseau's old red banquet I ate his violin
great party at the Bateau Lavoir riot mentioned in the textbooks
     of Algeria
Tzara in the Bois de Boulogne explaining the alchemy of the
     machineguns of the cuckoos
he weeps translating me into Swedish
well dressed in a violet tie and black pants
a sweet purple beard which emerged from his face like the moss
     hanging from the walls of Anarchism
he spoke endlessly of his quarrels with André Breton
whom he had helped one day trim his golden mustache
old Blaise Cendrars received me into his study and spoke wearily
     of the enormous length of Siberia
Jacques Vaché invited me to inspect his terrible collection of
     pistols
poor Cocteau saddened by the once marvelous Radiguet at his
     last thought I fainted
Rigaut with a letter of introduction to Death
and Gide praised the telephone and other remarkable inventions
we agreed in principle though he gossiped of lavender underwear
but for all that he drank deeply of the grass of Whitman and
     was intrigued by all lovers named Colorado
princes of America arriving with their armfuls of shrapnel and
     baseball
Oh Guillaume the world so easy to fight seemed so easy
did you know the great political classicists would invade Mont-
     parnasse

with not one sprig of prophetic laurel to green their foreheads
not one pulse of green in their pillows no leaf left from their
  wars — Mayakovsky arrived and revolted

III

Came back sat on a tomb and stared at your rough menhir
a piece of thin granite like an unfinished phallus
a cross fading into the rock 2 poems on the stone one Coeur
  Renversée
other Habituez-vous comme moi A ces prodiges que j'annonce
  Guillaume Apollinaire de Kostrowitsky
someone placed a jam bottle filled with daisies and a 5&10c.
  surrealist typist ceramic rose
happy little tomb with flowers and overturned heart
under a fine mossy tree beneath which I sat snaky trunk
summer boughs and leaves umbrella over the menhir and nobody
  there
Et quelle voix sinistre ulule Guillaume qu'es-tu devenu
his nextdoor neighbor is a tree
there underneath the crossed bones heaped and yellow cranium
  perhaps
and the printed poems Alcools in my pocket his voice in the
  museum
Now middleage footsteps walk the gravel
a man stares at the name and moves toward the crematory
  building
same sky rolls over thru clouds as Mediterranean days on the
  Riviera during war

drinking Apollo in love eating occasional opium he'd taken the
    light

One must have felt the shock in St. Germain when he went out
    Jacob & Picasso coughing in the dark

a bandage unrolled and the skull left still on a bed outstretched
    pudgy fingers the mystery and ego gone

a bell tolls in the steeple down the street birds warble in the
    chestnut trees

Famille Bremont sleeps nearby Christ hangs big chested and
    sexy in their tomb

my cigarette smokes in my lap and fills the page with smoke and
    flames

an ant runs over my corduroy sleeve the tree I lean on grows
    slowly

bushes and branches upstarting through the tombs one silky
    spiderweb gleaming on granite

I am buried here and sit by my grave beneath a tree

THE LION FOR REAL

"Soyez muette pour moi, Idole contemplative . . ."

I came home and found a lion in my living room
Rushed out on the fire-escape screaming Lion! Lion!
Two stenographers pulled their brunette hair and banged the
    window shut
I hurried home to Paterson and stayed two days.

Called up my old Reichian analyst
who'd kicked me out of therapy for smoking marijuana
'It's happened' I panted There's a Lion in my room'
'I'm afraid any discussion would have no value' he hung up.

I went to my old boyfriend we got drunk with his girlfriend
I kissed him and announced I had a lion with a mad gleam in
    my eye
We wound up fighting on the floor I bit his eyebrow & he
    kicked me out
I ended masturbating in his jeep parked in the street moaning
    'Lion.'

Found Joey my novelist friend and roared at him 'Lion!'
He looked at me interested and read me his spontaneous ignu
    high poetries
I listened for lions all I heard was Elephant Tiglon Hippogryph
    Unicorn Ants
But figured he really understood me when we made it in Ignaz
    Wisdom's bathroom.

But next day he sent me a leaf from his Smokey Mountain retreat
'I love you little Bo-Bo with your delicate golden lions
But there being no Self and No Bars therefore the Zoo of your
    dear Father hath no Lion
You said your mother was mad don't expect me to produce
    the Monster for your Bridegroom.'

Confused dazed and exalted bethought me of real lion starved
    in his stink in Harlem
Opened the door the room was filled with the bomb blast of
    his anger
He roaring hungrily at the plaster walls but nobody could hear
    him outside thru the window
My eye caught the edge of the red neighbor apartment building
    standing in deafening stillness

We gazed at each other his implacable yellow eye in the red
    halo of fur
Waxed rheumy on my own but he stopped roaring and bared a
    fang greeting.
I turned my back and cooked broccoli for supper on an iron
    gas stove
boilt water and took a hot bath in the old tub under the sink
    board.

He didn't eat me, tho I regretted him starving in my presence.
Next week he wasted away a sick rug full of bones wheaten
    hair falling out
enraged and reddening eye as he lay aching huge hairy head on
    his paws
by the egg-crate bookcase filled up with thin volumes of Plato,
    & Buddha.

Sat by his side every night averting my eyes from his hungry
    motheaten face
stopped eating myself he got weaker and roared at night while
    I had nightmares
Eaten by lion in bookstore on Cosmic Campus, a lion myself
    starved by Professor Kandisky, dying in a lion's flophouse
    circus,
I woke up mornings the lion still added dying on the floor—
    'Terrible Presence!' I cried 'Eat me or die!'

It got up that afternoon—walked to the door with its paw on
    the wall to steady its trembling body
Let out a soul rending creak from the bottomless roof of his
    mouth
thundering from my floor to heaven heavier than a volcano at
    night in Mexico
Pushed the door open and said in a gravelly voice "Not this time
    Baby—but I will be back again.'

Lion that eats my mind now for a decade knowing only your
    hunger
Not the bliss of your satisfaction O roar of the Universe how
    am I chosen
In this life I have heard your promise I am ready to die I have
    served
Your starved and ancient Presence O Lord I wait in my room
    at your Mercy.

Paris 1958

IGNU

On top of that if you know me I pronounce you an ignu

Ignu knows nothing of the world

a great ignoramus in factories though he may own or inspire
them or even be production manager

Ignu has knowledge of the angel indeed ignu is angel in comical
form

W. C. Fields Harpo Marx ignus Whitman an ignu

Rimbaud a natural ignu in his boy pants

The ignu may be queer though like not kind ignu blows arch-
angels for the strange thrill

a gnostic women love him Christ overflowed with trembling
semen for many a dead aunt

He's a great cocksman most beautiful girls are worshipped by
ignu

Hollywood dolls or lone Marys of Idaho long-legged publicity
women and secret housewives

have known ignu in another lifetime and remember their lover

Husbands also are secretly tender to ignu their buddy

oldtime friendship can do anything cuckold bugger drunk
trembling and happy

Ignu lives only once and eternally and knows it

he sleeps in everybody's bed everyone's lonesome for ignu ignu
knew solitude early

So ignu's a primitive of cock and mind

equally the ignu has written liverish tomes personal metaphysics
abstract

images that scratch the moon 'lightningflash-flintspark' naked
lunch fried shoes adios king

The shadow of the angel is waving in the opposite direction

dawn of intelligence turns the telephones into strange animals he attacks the rose garden with his mystical shears snip snip snip

Ignu has painted Park Avenue with his own long melancholy

and ignu giggles in a hard chair over tea in Paris bald in his
decaying room a black hotel

Ignu with his wild mop walks by Coliseum weeping

he plucks a clover from Keats' grave & Shelley's a blade of grass

knew Coleridge they had slow hung-up talks at midnight over
tables of mahogany in London

sidestreet rooms in wintertime rain outside fog the cabman
blows his hand

Charles Dickens is born ignu hears the wail of the babe

Ignu goofs nights under bridges and laughs at battleships

ignu is a battleship without guns in the North Sea lost O the
flowerness of the moment

he knows geography he was there before he'll get out and die
already

reborn a bearded humming Jew of Arabian mournful jokes

man with a star on his forehead and halo over his cranium

listening to music musing happy at the fall of a leaf the moon-
light of immortality in his hair

table-hopping most elegant comrade of all most delicate man-
nered in the Sufi court

he wasn't even there at all

wearing zodiacal blue sleeves and the long peaked conehat of a
magician

harkening to the silence of a well at midnight under a red star

in the lobby of Rockefeller Center attentive courteous bare-eyed
enthusiastic with or without pants

he listens to jazz as if he were a negro afflicted with jewish
melancholy and white divinity

Ignu's a natural you can see it when he pays the cabfare
abstracted

pulling off the money from an impossible saintly roll

or counting his disappearing pennies to give to the strange bus-
      driver whom he admires
Ignu has sought you out he's the seeker of God
and God breaks down the world for him every ten years
he sees lightning flash in empty daylight when the sky is blue
he hears Blake's disembodied Voice recite the Sunflower in a
      room in Harlem
No woe on him surrounded by 700 thousand mad scholars moths
      fly out of his sleeve
He wants to die give up go mad break through into Eternity
live on and teach an aged saint or break down to an eyebrow
      clown
All ignus know each other in a moment's talk and measure each
      other up at once
as lifetime friends romantic winks and giggles across continents
sad moment paying the cab goodby and speeding away uptown
One or two grim ignus in the pack
one laughing monk in dungarees
one delighted by cracking his eggs in an egg cup
one chews gum to music all night long rock and roll
one anthropologist cuckoo in the Petén Rainforest
one sits in jail all year and bets karmaic racetrack
one chases girls down East Broadway into the horror movie
one pulls out withered grapes and rotten onions from his pants
one has a nannygoat under his bed to amuse visitors plasters the
      wall with his crap
collects scorpions whiskies skies etc. would steal the moon if he
      could find it
That would set fire to America but none of these make ignu
it's the soul that makes the style the tender firecracker of his
      thought

the amity of letters from strange cities to old friends
and the new radiance of morning on a foreign bed
A comedy of personal being his grubby divinity
Eliot probably an ignu one of the few who's funny when he eats
Williams of Paterson a dying American ignu
Burroughs a purest ignu his haircut is a cream his left finger
    pinkie chopped off for early ignu reasons metaphysical spells love
        spells with psychoanalysts
his very junkhood an accomplishment beyond a million dollars
Celine himself an old ignu over prose
I saw him in Paris dirty old gentleman of ratty talk
with longhaired cough three wormy sweaters round his neck
brown mould under historic fingernails
pure genius his giving morphine all night to 1400 passengers on
        a sinking ship
'because they were all getting emotional'
Who's amazing you is ignu communicate with me
by mail post telegraph phone street accusation or scratching at
        my window
and send me a true sign I'll reply special delivery
DEATH IS A LETTER THAT WAS NEVER SENT
Knowledge born of stamps words coins pricks jails seasons sweet
        ambition laughing gas
history with a gold halo photographs of the sea painting a
        celestial din in the bright window
one eye in a black cloud
and the lone vulture on a sand plain seen from the window of a
        Turkish bus
It must be a trick. Two diamonds in the hand one Poetry one
        Charity

proves we have dreamed and the long sword of intelligence
over which I constantly stumble like my pants at the age six—
     embarrassed.

NY 1958

DEATH TO VAN GOGH'S EAR!

POET is Priest

Money has reckoned the soul of America

Congress broken thru to the precipice of Eternity

the President built a War machine which will vomit and rear up
Russia out of Kansas

The American Century betrayed by a mad Senate which no
longer sleeps with its wife

Franco has murdered Lorca the fairy son of Whitman

just as Mayakovsky committed suicide to avoid Russia

Hart Crane distinguished Platonist committed suicide to cave in
the wrong America

just as millions of tons of human wheat were burned in secret
caverns under the White House

while India starved and screamed and ate mad dogs full of rain

and mountains of eggs were reduced to white powder in the halls
of Congress

no godfearing man will walk there again because of the stink of
the rotten eggs of America

and the Indians of Chiapas continue to gnaw their vitaminless
tortillas

aborigines of Australia perhaps gibber in the eggless wilderness

and I rarely have an egg for breakfast tho my work requires
infinite eggs to come to birth in Eternity

eggs should be eaten or given to their mothers

and the grief of the countless chickens of America is expressed
in the screaming of her comedians over the radio

Detroit has built a million automobiles of rubber trees and
phantoms

but I walk, I walk, and the Orient walks with me, and all Africa
walks

and sooner or later North America will walk

for as we have driven the Chinese Angel from our door he will
drive us from the Golden Door of the future

we have not cherished pity on Tanganyika

Einstein alive was mocked for his heavenly politics

Bertrand Russell driven from New York for getting laid

and the immortal Chaplin has been driven from our shores with
the rose in his teeth

a secret conspiracy by Catholic Church in the lavatories of
Congress has denied contraceptives to the unceasing
masses of India.

Nobody publishes a word that is not the cowardly robot ravings
of a depraved mentality

the day of the publication of the true literature of the American
body will be day of Revolution

the revolution of the sexy lamb

the only bloodless revolution that gives away corn

poor Genet will illuminate the harvesters of Ohio

Marijuana is a benevolent narcotic but J. Edgar Hoover prefers
his deathly scotch

And the heroin of Lao-Tze & the Sixth Patriarch is punished
by the electric chair

but the poor sick junkies have nowhere to lay their heads

fiends in our government have invented a cold-turkey cure for
addiction as obsolete as the Defense Early Warning Radar
System.

I am the defense early warning radar system

I see nothing but bombs

I am not interested in preventing Asia from being Asia

and the governments of Russia and Asia will rise and fall but
Asia and Russia will not fall

the government of America also will fall but how can America
   fall
I doubt if anyone will ever fall anymore except governments
fortunately all the governments will fall
the only ones which won't fall are the good ones
and the good ones don't yet exist
But they have to begin existing they exist in my poems
they exist in the death of the Russian and American governments
they exist in the death of Hart Crane & Mayakovsky
Now is the time for prophecy without death as a consequence
the universe will ultimately disappear
Hollywood will rot on the windmills of Eternity
Hollywood whose movies stick in the throat of God
Yes Hollywood will get what it deserves
Time
Seepage of nerve-gas over the radio
History will make this poem prophetic and its awful silliness a
   hideous spiritual music
I have the moan of doves and the feather of ecstasy
Man cannot long endure the hunger of the cannibal abstract
War is abstract
the world will be destroyed
but I will die only for poetry, that will save the world
Monument to Sacco & Vanzetti not yet financed to ennoble
   Boston
natives of Kenya tormented by idiot con-men from England
South Africa in the grip of the white fool
Vachel Lindsay Secretary of the Interior
Poe Secretary of Imagination
Pound Secty. Economics
and Kra belongs to Kra, and Pukti to Pukti
crossfertilization of Blok and Artaud

Van Gogh's Ear on the currency
no more propaganda for monsters
and poets should stay out of politics or become monsters
I have become monstrous with politics
the Russian poet undoubtedly monstrous in his secret notebook
Tibet should be left alone
These are obvious prophecies
America will be destroyed
Russian poets will struggle with Russia
Whitman warned against this `fabled Damned of nations'
Where was Theodore Roosevelt when he sent out ultimatums
    from his castle in Camden
Where was the House of Representatives when Crane read aloud
    from his prophetic books
What was Wall Street scheming when Lindsay announced the
    doom of Money
Were they listening to my ravings in the locker rooms of Bick-
    fords Employment Offices?
Did they bend their ears to the moans of my soul when I
    struggled with market research statistics in the Forum at
    Rome?
No they were fighting in fiery offices, on carpets of heartfailure,
    screaming and bargaining with Destiny
fighting the Skeleton with sabres, muskets, buck teeth, indigestion,
    bombs of larceny, whoredom, rockets, pederasty,
back to the wall to build up their wives and apartments, lawns,
    suburbs, fairydoms,
Puerto Ricans crowded for massacre on 114th St. for the sake
    of an imitation Chinese-Moderne refrigerator
Elephants of mercy murdered for the sake of an Elizabethan
    birdcage

millions of agitated fanatics in the bughouse for the sake of the
    screaming soprano of industry

Money-chant of soapers—toothpaste apes in television sets—
    deodorizers on hypnotic chairs—

petroleum mongers in Texas—jet plane streaks among the
    clouds—

sky writers liars in the face of Divinity—fanged butchers of
    hats and shoes, all Owners! Owners! Owners! with
    obsession on property and vanishing Selfhood!

and their long editorials on the fence of the screaming negro
    attacked by ants crawled out of the front page!

Machinery of a mass electrical dream! A war-creating Whore of
    Babylon bellowing over Capitols and Academies!

Money! Money! Money! shrieking mad celestial money of
    illusion! Money made of nothing, starvation, suicide!
    Money of failure! Money of death!

Money against Eternity! and eternity's strong mills grind out
    vast paper of Illusion!

Paris 1958

LAUGHING GAS

To Gary Snyder
The red tin begging cup you gave me,
I lost it but its contents are undisturbed.

I

High on Laughing Gas
I've been here before
the odd vibration of
the same old universe

the nasal whine of the dentist's drill
        singing against the nostalgic
            piano Muzak in the wall
insistent, familiar, penetrating
    the teeth, where've I heard that
        asshole jazz before?

The universe is a void
in which there is a dreamhole
The dream disappears
        the hole closes

It's the instant of going
into or coming out of
existence that is
important—to catch on
to the secret of the magic
    box

Stepping outside the universe
    by means of Nitrous Oxide
anesthetizing mind-consciousness

    the chiliasm was an impersonal dream —
one of many, being mere dreams.

    the sadness of birth
    and death, the sadness of
changing from dream to dream,
the constant farewell
of forms . . .
        saying ungoodby to what
didn't exist

The many worlds that don't exist
all which seem real
all joke
all lost cartoon

At that moment the whole goofy-spooky of the Universe
WHAT?! Joke Being slips into Nothing like the tail of a lizard
disappearing into a crack in the Wall with the final receding
eyehole ending Loony Tunes accompanied by Woody Wood-
pecker's hindoo maniac laughter in the skull. Nobody gets hurt.
They all disappear. They were never there. Beginningless per-
fection.

    That's why Satori's accompanied by laughter
    and the Zenmaster rips up the Sutras in fury.

And the pain of this contrariety
The cycles of scream and laughter
faces and asses Christs and Buddhas
each with his own universe dragged
over the snowy mental poles
like a sack mad Santa Clauses
Worst pain in the dentist's chair comes true
novocain also arrives in the cycle
every hap will have its chance
even God will come Once or Twice
Satan will be my personal enemy

Relax and die—
The process will repeat itself
Be Born! Be Born!
Back to the same old smiling
                              dentist—

The Bloomfield police car
        with its idiot red light
        revolving on its head
        balefully at Eternity
                    gone in an instant
                    —simultaneous
                    appearance of Bankrobbers
        at the Twentieth Century Bank
The fire engines screaming
        toward an old lady's
        burned-in-her-bedroom
        today apocalypse
            tomorrow
        Mickey Mouse cartoons—

I'm disgusted! it's Unbelievable!
What a funny horrible
    dirty joke!
The whole universe a shaggy dog story!
      with a weird ending that begins again
        till you get the point
'It was a dark and gloomy night . . .'
      'in every direction in and
        out'
          'You take the high road
     and I'll take the low'
              —everybody lost
in Scotlands of mind-consciousness—

      Adonoi Echad!
It is not One, but Two,
    not two but Infinite—
the universe be born and die
    in endless series in the mind!

Gary Snyder, Jack, Zen thinkers
    split open existence
    and laugh & Cry—
what's shock? what's measure?
    when the Mind's an irrational
      traffic light in
        Gobi—
follow the blinking lights of contrariety!

What's the use avoiding rats
and horror, hiding from Cops
    and dentists' drills?
Somebody will invent
    a Buchenwald next door
—an ant's dream's
    funnier than
        ours
—he has more of them
    faster and seems
    to give less of
      a shit—

O waves of probable
    and improbable
Universes—
    Everybody's right

I'll finish this poem
    in my next life.

II

. . . . with eye opening
slowly to perceive
that I be coming out
    of a trance—
one look at the lipstick
    it's a nurse
in a dentist's office

    that first frog
thought leaping out of
    the void

    . . . a glimpse
out of which the whole
process unfolds this
universe & logically
and symmetrically next
unbuilds it in exact
reverse till you arrive
back at the Nothing
in which one chance
note was originally
struck . . .

    , the Chardash
of Creation, the first banal chord
establishing Music forever in
    its mechanical jukebox

        . . . and the whole
    structure unfolds
itself inevitably and
        folds back into
Nothing again . . .

        —the same man
crossing the street looking
both ways watch out for
the cars—

and each time, returning
with a jerk of the face
('praps a dental touch)
dictated by the sinking
sensation, Oof! I've
been hoodwinked—

        again like
    someone in the Circus
defying death, got thrown
        into the orchestra—
            Note the music blaring
with an indifferent flourish of Triumph
        a nightmare Razz
        —as the acrobat leaps
out into the void—

Me! I made that Last Chance
jump off the wire
way high up in the Big Top
long ago . . .
it's happening again!

I wake up dazed...

it being the dream
of someone in a dentist's
chair in a Universe he
imagines — coming out
of gas —
it's only happening
in the closed universe of
illusion

III

A nice day in the Universe on Broad Street—sun shines today as it never shone before and never will again—stillness in the blue sky—the church's gold dome across the park sending and receiving flashes of light—I feel heart sick to destroy this all—

What hope have the children in their prams passing the white silent doors of the houses—only the Public Library knows.

Premonition in the dentist's chair—mechanical voices over the radio singing Destination Moon—mysterious sorrow for the moon of this forgotten universe—humans, singing, singing—of the moon—for money?—except it's the imbecilic canned voice of eternity rocking & rolling in Space making invisible announcements—

The Doc's agreed to the experiment—novocain, my mouth's begun to disappear first—like the Cheshire Cat.

BACK: Endless cycles of conflict happening in nothingness
make it impossible to grasp for the perfection
which does not exist
but is not necessary
so everything is final and occurs over & over again
till we will finally blank out as expected.

The First Note of Creation:
the only one there could be if there
weren't nothing but
an idea that there might
not be nothing—

Sherman Adams will resign
I'm holding my breath
the shiver run thru my belly
the nurse will be singing I love you
between breaths the Buddhists are right
a tear
siffle in the cheek
the possibility escape
the eye glare thru glasses
Nothing grasped at & ungrasped as its trance thought passes

I take my pen in hand
The same old way sings Sinatra
I'm writing to You give me understanding
I pray sings Sinatra
Can I never glimpse the round we have made?
Write me as soon as able sings Sinatra
O Lord burn me out of existence.

You've got a long body sings Sinatra
I refuse to breathe and return to form
I've seen every moment in advance before
I've turned my neck a million times
                    & written this note
                & been greeted with fire and cheers
I refuse to stop
                —thinking—
What Perfection has escaped me?

An endless cycle of possibilities clashing in Nothing
with each mistake in the writing inevitable from the beginning
            of time

The doctor's phone number is Pilgrim 1-0000
Are you calling me, Nothing?

The universe be smashed
to smithereens by the oncoming
atomic explosions with
Eisenhower as once President
of a place called U.S.
Gregory wrote the Bomb!
Russians dream of Mars &
when the cosmos goes and
all consciousness after the
final explosion of imagination
in the void it won't have
made any difference that it
all both did and did not
happen, whatever it was once
thought to he so real—
it will be—gone.

O that I might die on the spot
I'll have to go back
any prophecy might have been right
it's all a great Exception

My bus will arrive as foretold
it's the end of another September
war is on the radio ahead
we are all going to the inevitable beauty of doom
a firebox stands sentient before the library
it's hot sun now I'm crazy scribbling
—It began abstract and mindless nowhere

planets of thought have passed
it'll end where it began

I want to return to normal
—but there is no changelessness
but in Nirvana
                    Or is there
Ever Rest, Lord?—and what sages
know and sit.
                    I'm a spy
in Bloomfield on a park bench
            —frightened by buses—

What's that bee doing hanging round my shoe? my borrowed
            and inevitable shoe?
A vast red truck moving with boxes of dead television sets in the
            back

American flag waving over the library

On the bus I sit by a negress

This is an explosion

IV

Back in the same old black hole
   where Possibility closes the
      last door
     and the Great void remains
    . . . a glass
in the dust reflecting the sun,
      fragment of a bottle
   that never knew it existed

          . . . under a tree
that sleeps all winter
    till it grows its eyes
        in May heat
and flowers upward with a thousand
      green sensations
dies, and forgets itself in Snow

   . . . Phantom in Phantom

If we didn't exist, God
would have to create this
to leave no room for complaint
   by any of the birds & bees
who might have missed their
     chance (to be)

Fate tells a big lie.

. . . And the big kind Dreamer
is on the nod again
        God sleeps!
He's in for a big surprise
one of his dreams is going to come true
        He'll get the answer too
        He'll get the answer too

Just a flash in the cosmic pan
—just an instant when there
        might have been a light
        had there been any pan
                to reflect it—

—we can lie on the bed and imagine
        ourselves away—

I'm afraid to stop breathing—
        first the pain in the
                body
        suffocation, then
                the Death.

V

The pain of gas flowing into the eye
the crooked tooth-drills hanging like gallows
on a miniature Jupiter
Thru the open window, spring frozen
in the young tree
the repeated bong of the doorbell
opening elsewhere
I've come back to the same medicine
cabinet in the universe — Bong,
I know I'm more real than the dentist!
a serious embarrassment, having grasped to one Self
though admittedly I'd seen it disappear
over and over

TRACKLESS TRANSIT CORPORATION

runs a bus thru Bloomfield
. . . blossoming
in the bottom of an unborn daisy
it will vanish into the Whist-not

History will keep repeating
itself forever like the woman
in the image on the Dutch Cleanser box

A way out of the mirror
was found by the image
that realized its existence
was only...
a stranger completely like myself

A way out for ever! has not been found
to enter the ground whence the images
        rise, and repeat themselves

————————————

The sadness is, that every leaf
        has fallen before—

At my feet an ant crawling
        in the broken asphalt—
and this exact white lollypop stick
        & twig of branch
lain next to that soggy match
        near those few grassblades...
and I've sat here and took this note
        before and tried to remember—
and now I do—remember what
I'm writing as I write it down
I know when I'm going to stop
I know when I'm forgetting and
know when I
        take a jump and change—
            Impossible
to do anything but right now in all
        the universe at once—
            which Art does, and
the Insight of Laughing Gas?

Ha Ha Ha Ha Ha
and the monk laughs
at the moon—
and everybody 10 miles round
in all directions wonders
why—he's just reminding
them—of what—of
the moon, the old dumb moon
of a million lives.

MESCALINE

Rotting Ginsberg, I stared in the mirror naked today
I noticed the old skull, I'm getting balder
my pate gleams in the kitchen light under thin hair
like the skull of some monk in old catacombs lighted by
a guard with flashlight
followed by a mob of tourists
so there is death
my kitten mews, and looks into the closet
Boito sings on the phonograph tonight his ancient song of
angels
Antinoüs bust in brown photograph still gazing down from
my wall
a light burst from God's delicate hand sends down a wooden
dove to the calm virgin
Beato Angelico's universe
the cat's gone mad and scraowls around the floor

What happens when the death gong hits rotting ginsberg on
the head
what universe do I enter
death death death death death the cat's at rest
are we ever free of—rotting ginsberg
Then let it decay, thank God I know
thank who
thank who
Thank you, O lord, beyond my eye
the path must lead somewhere
the path
the path
flint the rotting shit dump, thru the Angelico orgies

Beep, emit a burst of babe and begone
perhaps that's the answer, wouldn't know till you had a kid
I dunno, never had a kid never will at the rate I'm going

Yes, I should be good, I should get married
find out what it's all about
but I can't stand these women all over me
smell of Naomi
erk, I'm stuck with this familiar rotting ginsberg
can't stand boys even anymore
can't stand
can't stand
and who wants to get fucked up the ass, really?
Immense seas passing over
the flow of time
and who wants to be famous and sign autographs like a movie
     star

I want to know
I want I want ridiculous *to know to know* WHAT rotting
     ginsberg
I want to know what happens after I rot
because I'm already rotting
my hair's falling out I've got a belly I'm sick of sex
my ass drags in the universe I know too much
and not enough
I want to know what happens after I die
well I'll find out soon enough
do I really need to know now?
is that any use at all use use use
death death death death death
god god god god god god god the Lone Ranger
the rhythm of the typewriter

What can I do to Heaven by pounding on Typewriter
I'm stuck change the record Gregory ah excellent he's doing
        just that
and I am too conscious of a million ears
at present creepy ears, making commerce
too many pictures in the newspapers
faded yellowed press clippings
I'm going away from the poem to be a drak contemplative

trash of the mind
trash of the world
man is half trash
all trash in the grave

What can Williams be thinking in Paterson, death so much on
        him
so soon so soon
Williams, what is death?
Do you face the great question now each moment
or do you forget at breakfast looking at your old ugly love in
        the face
are you prepared to be reborn
to give release to this world to enter a heaven
or give release, give release
and all be done—and see a lifetime—all eternity gone
        over
into naught, a trick question proposed by the moon to the
        answerless earth
No Glory for man! No Glory for man! No glory for me!
        No me!

No point writing when the spirit doth not lead

NY 1959

LYSERGIC ACID

It is a multiple million eyed monster
it is hidden in all its elephants and selves
it hummeth in the electric typewriter
it is electricity connected to itself, if it hath wires
it is a vast Spiderweb
and I am on the last millionth infinite tentacle of the spiderweb,
      a worrier
lost, separated, a worm, a thought, a self
one of the millions of skeletons of China
one of the particular mistakes
I alien Ginsberg a separate consciousness
I who want to be God
I who want to hear the infinite minutest vibration of eternal
      harmony
I who wait trembling my destruction by that aethereal music
      in the fire
I who hate God and give him a name
I who make mistakes on the eternal typewriter
I who am Doomed

But at the far end of the universe the million eyed Spyder that
      hath no name
spinneth of itself endlessly
the monster that is no monster approaches with apples, perfume,
      railroads, television, skulls
a universe that eats and drinks itself
blood from my skull
Tibetan creature with hairy breast and Zodiac on my stomach
this sacrificial victim unable to have a good time

My face in the mirror, thin hair, blood congested in streaks down
      beneath my eyes, cocksucker, a decay, a talking lust
a snaeap, a snarl, a tic of consciousness in infinity
a creep in the eyes of all Universes
trying to escape my Being, unable to pass on to the Eye
I vomit, I am in a trance, my body is seized in convulsion, my
      stomach crawls, water from my mouth, I am here in
      Inferno
dry bones of myriad lifeless mummies naked on the web, the
      Ghosts, I am a Ghost
I cry out where I am in the music, to the room, to whomever
      near, you, Are you God?
No, do you want me to be God?
Is there no Answer?
Must there always be an Answer? you reply,
and were it up to me to say Yes or No
Thank God I am not God! Thank God I am not God!
But that I long for a Yes of Harmony to penetrate
to every corner of the universe, under every condition whatsoever
a Yes there Is . . . a Yes I Am . . . a Yes You Are . . . a We

A We
and that must be an It, and a They, and a Thing with No
      Answer
It creepeth, it waiteth, it is still, it is begun, it is the Horns of
      Battle it is Multiple Sclerosis
it is not my hope
it is not my death at Eternity
it is not my word, not poetry
beware my Word

It is a Ghost Trap, woven by priest in Sikkim or Tibet
a crossframe on which a thousand threads of differing color
are strung, a spiritual tennis racket
in which when I look I see aethereal lightwaves radiate
bright energy passing round on the threads as for billions of years
the thread-bands magically changing hues one transformed to
      another as if the
Ghost Trap
were an image of the Universe in miniature
conscious sentient part of the interrelated machine
making waves outward in Time to the Beholder
displaying its own image in miniature once for all
repeated minutely downward with endless variations throughout
      all of itself
it being all the same in every part

This image or energy which reproduces itself at the depths of
      space from the very Beginning
in what might be an O or an Aum
and trailing variations made of the same Word circles round
      itself in the same pattern as its original Appearance
creating a larger Image of itself throughout depths of Time
outward circling thru bands of faroff Nebulae & vast Astrologies
contained, to be true to itself, in a Mandala painted on an
      Elephant's hide,
or in a photograph of a painting on the side of an imaginary
      Elephant which smiles, tho how the Elephant looks is an
      irrelevant joke —
it might be a Sign held by a Flaming Demon, or Ogre of
      Transcience,
or in a photograph of my own belly in the void
or in my eye
or in the eye of the monk who made the Sign

or in its own Eye that stares on Itself at last and dies

and tho an eye can die
and tho my eye can die
the billion-eyed monster, the Nameless, the Answerless, the
    Hidden-from-me, the endless Being
one creature that gives birth to itself
thrills in its minutest particular, sees out of all eyes differently
    at once
One and not One moves on its own ways
I cannot follow

And I have made an image of the monster here
and I will make another
it feels like Cryptozoids
it creeps and undulates beneath the sea
it is coming to take over the city
it invades beneath every Consciousness
it is delicate as the Universe
it makes me vomit
because I am afraid I will miss its appearance
it appears anyway
it appears anyway in the mirror
it washes out of the mirror like the sea
it is myrìad undulations
it washes out of the mirror and drowns the beholder
it drowns the world when it drowns the world
it drowns in itself
it floats outward like a corpse filled with music
the noise of war in its head
a babe laugh in its belly
a scream of agony in the dark sea
a smile on the lips of a blind statue
it was there

it was not mine
I wanted to use it for myself
to be heroic
but it is not for sale to this consciousness
it goes its own way forever
it will complete all creatures
it will be the radio of the future
it will hear itself in time
it wants a rest
it is tired of hearing and seeing itself
it wants another form another victim
it wants me
it gives me good reason
it gives me reason to exist
it gives me endless answers
a consciousness to be separate and a consciousness to see
I am beckoned to be One or the other, to say I am both and
        be neither
it can take care of itself without me
it is Both Answerless (it answers not to that name)
it hummeth on the electric typewriter
it types a fragmentary word which is
a fragmentary word,

MANDALA

Gods dance on their own bodies
New flowers open forgetting Death
Celestial eyes beyond the heartbreak of illusion
I see the gay Creator
Bands rise up in anthem to the worlds

Flags and banners waving in transcendence
One image in the end remains myriad-eyed in Eternity
This is the Work! This is the Knowledge! This is the End
    of man!

S.F. June 2, 1959

MAGIC PSALM

Because this world is on the wing and what cometh no man
    can know

O Phantom that my mind pursues from year to year descend
    from heaven to this shaking flesh

catch up my fleeting eye in the vast Ray that knows no bounds
    —Inseparable—Master—

Giant outside Time with all its falling leaves—Genius of the
    Universe—Magician in Nothingness where appear red
    clouds—

Unspeakable King of the roads that are gone—Unintelligible
    Horse riding out of the graveyard—Sunset spread over
    Cordillera and insect—Gnarl Moth—

Griever—Laugh with no mouth, Heart that never had flesh to
    die—Promise that was not made—Reliever, whose
    blood burns in a million animals wounded—

O Mercy, Destroyer of the World, O Mercy, Creator of Breasted
    Illusions, O Mercy, cacophonous warmouthed doveling,
    Come,

invade my body with the sex of God, choke up my nostrils with
    corruption's infinite caress,

transfigure me to slimy worms of pure sensate transcendency
    I'm still alive,

croak my voice with uglier than reality, a psychic tomato
    speaking Thy million mouths,

Myriad-tongued my Soul, Monster or Angel, Lover that comes
    to fuck me forever—white gown on the Eyeless Squid—

Asshole of the Universe into which I disappear—Elastic Hand
    that spoke to Crane—Music that passes into the phono-
    graph of years from another Millennium—Ear of the

buildings of NY—

That which I believe—have seen—seek endlessly in leaf dog
   eye—fault always, lack—which makes me think—

Desire that created me, Desire I hide in my body, Desire all
   Man know Death, Desire surpassing the Babylonian pos-
   sible world

that makes my flesh shake orgasm of Thy Name which I don't
   know never will never speak—

Speak to Mankind to say the great bell tolls a golden tone on
   iron balconies in every million universe,

I am Thy prophet come home this world to scream an unbear-
   able Name thru my 5 senses hideous sixth

that knows Thy Hand on its invisible phallus, covered with
   electric bulbs of death—

Peace, Resolver where I mess up illusion, Softmouth Vagina
   that enters my brain from above, Ark-Dove with a bough
   of Death.

Drive me crazy, God I'm ready for disintegration of my mind,
   disgrace me in the eye of the earth,

attack my hairy heart with terror eat my cock Invisible croak
   of deathfrog leap on me pack of heavy dogs salivating
   light,

devour my brain One flow of endless consciousness, I'm scared
   of your promise must make scream my prayer in fear—

Descend O Light Creator & Eater of Mankind, disrupt the
   world in its madness of bombs and murder,

Volcanos of flesh over London, on Paris a rain of eyes—truck-
   loads of angelhearts besmearing Kremlin walls—the
   skullcup of light to New York—

myriad jeweled feet on the terraces of Pekin—veils of electrical
   gas descending over India—cities of Bacteria invading

the brain—the Soul escaping into the rubber waving mouths of Paradise—

This is the Great Call, this is the Tocsin of the Eternal War, this is the cry of Mind slain in Nebulae,

this is the Golden Bell of the Church that has never existed, this is the Boom in the heart of the sunbeam, this is the trumpet of the Worm at Death,

Appeal of the handless castrate grab Alm golden seed of Futurity thru the quake & volcan of the world—

Shovel my feet under the Andes, splatter my brains on the Sphinx, drape my beard and hair over Empire State Building,

cover my belly with hands of moss, fill up my ears with your lightning, blind me with prophetic rainbows

That I taste the shit of Being at last, that I touch Thy genitals in the palmtree,

that the vast Ray of Futurity enter my mouth to sound Thy Creation Forever Unborn, O Beauty invisible to my Century!

that my prayer surpass my understanding, that I lay my vanity at Thy foot, that I no longer fear Judgment over Allen of this world

born in Newark come into Eternity in New York crying again in Peru for human Tongue to psalm the Unspeakable,

that I surpass desire for transcendency and enter the calm water of the universe

that I ride out this wave, not drown forever in the flood of my imagination

that I not be slain thru my own insane magic, this crime be punished in merciful jails of Death,

men understand my speech out of their own Turkish heart,
    the prophets aid me with Proclamation,
the Seraphim acclaim Thy Name, Thyself at once in one huge
    Mouth of Universe make meat reply.

1960

THE REPLY

God answers with my doom! I am annulled
           this poetry blanked from the fiery ledger
   my lies be answered by the worm at my ear
  my visions by the hand falling over my eyes to cover them
            from sight of my skeleton
  my longing to be God by the trembling bearded jaw flesh
       that covers my skull like monster-skin
     Stomach vomiting out the soul-vine, cadaver on
      the floor of a bamboo hut, body-meat crawling toward
      its fate nightmare rising in my brain
The noise of the drone of creation adoring its Slayer, the yowp
        of birds to the Infinite, dogbarks like the sound
  of vomit in the air, frogs croaking Death at trees
I am a Seraph and I know not whither I go into the Void
I am a man and I know not whither I go into Death — —
                Christ Christ poor hopeless
      lifted on the Cross between Dimension—
     to see the Ever-Unknowable!
a dead gong shivers thru all flesh and a vast Being enters my
    brain from afar that lives forever
    None but the Presence too mighty to record! the Presence
    in Death, before whom I am helpless
       makes me change from Allen to a skull
Old One-Eye of dreams in which I do not wake but die—
    hands pulled into the darkness by a frightful Hand
      —the worm's blind wriggle, cut—the plough
       is God himself
What ball of monster darkness from before the universe come
  back to visit me with blind command!

and I can blank out this consciousness, escape back
to New York love, and will
Poor pitiable Christ afraid of the foretold Cross,
Never to die—
Escape, but not forever—the Presence will come, the hour
will come, a strange truth enter the universe, death
show its Being as before
and I'll despair that *I forgot! forgot!* my fate return,
tho die of it—
What's sacred when the Thing is all the universe?
creeps to every soul like a vampire-organ singing behind
moonlit clouds—
poor being come squat
under bearded stars in a dark field in Peru
to drop my load—I'll die in horror that I die!
Not dams or pyramids but death, and we to prepare for that
nakedness, poor bones sucked dry by His long mouth
of ants and wind, & our souls murdered to prepare
His Perfection!
The moment's come, He's made His will revealed forever
and no flight into old Being further than the stars will not
find terminal in the same dark swaying port
of unbearable music
No refuge in Myself, which is on fire
or in the World which is His also to bomb & Devour!
Recognize His might! Loose hold
of my hands—my frightened skull
—for I had chose self-love—
my eyes, my nose, my face, my cock, my soul—and now
the faceless Destroyer!
A billion doors to the same new Being!

The universe turns inside out to devour me!
and the mighty burst of music comes from out the inhuman

door—

1960

THE END

I am I, old Father Fisheye that begat the ocean, the worm at my
    own ear, the serpent turning around a tree,
I sit in the mind of the oak and hide in the rose, I know if any
    wake up, none but my death,
come to me bodies, come to me prophecies, come all foreboding,
    come spirits and visions,
I receive all, I'll die of cancer, I enter the coffin forever, I close
    my eye, I disappear,
I fall on myself in winter snow, I roll in a great wheel through
    rain, I watch fuckers in convulsion,
car screech, furies groaning their basso music, memory fading
    in the brain, men imitating dogs,
I delight in a woman's belly, youth stretching his breasts and
    thighs to sex, the cock sprung inward
gassing its seed on the lips of Yin, the beasts dance in Siam,
    they sing opera in Moscow,
my boys yearn at dusk on stoops, I enter New York, I play my
    jazz on a Chicago Harpsichord,
Love that bore me I bear back to my Origin with no loss, I float
    over the vomiter
thrilled with my deathlessness, thrilled with this endlessness I
    dice and bury,
come Poet shut up eat my word, and taste my mouth in your ear.

NY 1960

Allen and Naomi Ginsberg, ca. 1935

SOME WORDS ON
ALLEN GINSBERG'S KADDISH

If only you knew
How your poet son, Allen,
Raves over the world,
Crazed for love of you!

—Louis Ginsberg
"To a Mother, Buried"

Allen Ginsberg was in his cozy, rose-covered cottage in Berkeley on June 9, 1956, when he received a telegram from his father telling him that his mother, Naomi, had died from a stroke in Pilgrim State Hospital on Long Island. As with all unexpected deaths, it came as a shock to Allen who had just celebrated his thirtieth birthday a few days earlier. Even though she had been lost to him for years as a result of her long descent into mental illness, he wasn't ready to say goodbye. "Tenderness and a tomb, the world is a tomb of tenderness. Life is a short flicker of love. Went out into the grass knelt down and cried a little—to heaven for her. Otherwise nothing," the stunned poet wrote in his journal at the time. "My childhood is gone with my mother."

Louis Ginsberg, Allen's father, told him it wasn't necessary for Allen to return for the burial. It wouldn't have been possible anyway, she was being buried the following afternoon and Allen was 3,000 miles away. Only a handful of people were at the cemetery for the interment, and there weren't enough men to have a *minyan*

Naomi Livergrant, ca. 1913

(a quorum of ten male Jewish adults required for public prayer). As a result, the traditional Jewish prayer for the dead, the Mourners' Kaddish, could not be recited.

Allen had just been posted to a ship that was sailing in a few days. His mission would be to take supplies to the DEW Line [Distant Early Warning] bases off the coast of Alaska during the short Arctic summertime. Waiting for his ship to weigh anchor, Allen wrote, "Everything changes toward death. My mother. Myself." He continued, "My childhood is gone with my mother. My memory becomes less clear. My body will go. There is no me left." After a few lines he stopped; he could not continue, it was all too fresh and painful. It would take him three years and several aborted tries to complete the poem he wanted to write for Naomi. It was to be his most personal poem and his most successful work of art. Although "Howl" is Ginsberg's most celebrated poem, "Kaddish" is certainly his greatest achievement.

There are two parts to the story of Ginsberg's "Kaddish." The first is Naomi's story, which ended with her death late that spring day in 1956. The second is the story of the creation of the poem itself, which began on the same day that her life ended.

Naomi's Story

Naomi Livergant was born in 1894 in the small town of Nevel, then part of the Pskov Oblast territory of Russia. Pskov Oblast bordered Estonia, Latvia, and Poland, and was part of the Pale, the area of western Russia where Jews were officially permitted to live. Sometimes exceptions were made, allowing Jews to live "beyond the pale," but Naomi's family was not granted that privilege. Her parents, Judith and Mendel Livergant, were little more than peasants subject to the whims of the Czar. When war broke out with Japan on Feb. 10, 1904, it seemed certain that her father, then twenty-nine years old, would be drafted into the Russian Army. Mendel, who made his living selling sewing machines, had a wife and four children to support, and he wasn't the least bit interested in going off to fight the Japanese. Like many others, he and his brother, Isser, decided to emigrate to America. They left their wives and children behind in Vitebsk, planning to send for them as soon as they were established in the new world.

By 1905 however, the frequency of the pogroms that ravaged the Jewish settlements in western Russia had reached a point where the family felt they had to leave. Judith Livergant fled with her four children; Elanor, Naomi, Max, and Sam, traveling with Isser's wife and her seven children. Once in America, the family adopted a new "Americanized" name, Mendel having already changed his name to Morris Levy at Ellis Island. By the time they arrived Morris was running his own candy store in the vicinity of Orchard Street on the Lower East Side, then the center of New York's Jewish ghetto. There, Morris busied himself making hand-churned ice cream sodas for those who could afford the luxury. It was on Orchard Street that Naomi remembered eating her first tomato, often believed to be poisonous by the poor European immigrants who had never seen the fruit before.

Within a few years, Morris decided to move the family to Newark, New Jersey, where, away from the over-crowding of the Lower East Side, he hoped they would enjoy a better life. Although the family was poor, Naomi was a bright student and attended Barringer High School, the best public school in the city. It was there, in 1912, that she met and began to date Louis Ginsberg, an intelligent, energetic boy about her same age. Louis was tall, dark-haired and wore glasses. The more reserved Louis proved to be a good match for the gregarious, feisty, free-spirited Naomi Levy. They had a good deal in common and both Naomi and Louis came from families interested in progressive politics. Naomi's family was from a region in Russia that was staunchly communist in ideology, while Louis' parents were influenced by socialist theory. That mix provided a great deal of spirited dinner conversations and debates.

After high school, Naomi completed two years at Newark Normal School, which qualified her to become a teacher. For a short time she taught kindergarten in the Newark public school system, where students remembered her as strict but pleasant. She moved on to teach remedial students in Woodbine, New Jersey, in order to be closer to Louis, who, after graduation from Rutgers had found a job teaching high school. Before long the two were engaged. Then in 1918, during the great influenza epidemic that swept Europe and America, Naomi's mother, Judith Levy died. The shock of her sudden death undoubtedly contributed to Naomi's first mental breakdown, which occurred the following year. She was incapacitated for several weeks and complained of a heightened sensitivity to sound and light that was nearly unbearable. She stayed in bed with the shades drawn, blocking out any external sound until eventually the problem went away. At the time, she and Louis thought it was a transient seizure and they continued to make plans for the wedding.

Louis' mother Rebecca, or Buba as the family called her, never really liked Naomi. She saw Naomi's mental breakdown as one more reason that Louis should not rush into marriage. Louis was unaware that the temporary case of hypersensitivity was a prelude to more serious mental problems. In spite of his mother's objections, he and Naomi were married in 1919 in Woodbine in a small ceremony held in a local mansion.

After the wedding, Naomi did not return to teaching and a year or so later the newlyweds moved back to Newark to live closer to their families. Louis found a good job teaching English to high school students in nearby Paterson, New Jersey, and for the next decade he commuted to school before the family relocated to Paterson permanently. Before long Naomi became pregnant, and on June 2, 1921, Naomi and Louis had their first son, who they named Eugene Brooks Ginsberg, after the great labor organizer and leader of the Socialist Party of America, Eugene V. Debs.

While living in Newark, Louis was able to turn his attention once more to his great avocation, poetry. He joined the Poetry Society of America and attended as many meetings as he could in New York City. There he became acquainted with some of the poets he most respected, Marianne Moore, Witter Bynner, and Wallace Stevens. Naomi would often go with him to the meetings and lectures in the city and it was on one of these visits to Greenwich Village that she met Maxwell Bodenheim, a well-known bohemian writer. Later, Naomi would claim that she had affairs with both Bodenheim and Clement Wood, another poet in their group. After the birth of Eugene, Naomi stayed closer to home and became more active in the local Communist Party. Still a free spirit, she often upset her fellow members by agitating for the inclusion of policies that promoted nudism or vegetarianism in the party platforms.

Eventually, the Ginsbergs moved to an apartment at 163 Quitman Street and, as time went by, Naomi became pregnant again. On June 3, 1926, she gave birth to her second son at Newark's Beth Israel Hospital. They named him Irwin Allen Ginsberg, but from the start they simply called him Allen. With two boys at home, Naomi seemed happy and content for a while. Her interest in party politics grew stronger and she took her young sons with her to the local meetings.

In 1929, when Allen was three, Naomi became ill and had to undergo pancreatic surgery. She nearly died during the operation, and the surgery left her with horrible scars that reminded Allen of "hideous thick zippers." Unable to care for the children after the operation, the family moved in with Naomi's sister Elanor and her husband Max Frohman. They stayed in the Bronx with the Frohman's for nearly six months while Naomi regained her strength. It was while she was recovering that Naomi suffered another nervous breakdown, this one far more serious than the first.

Naomi was taken to Bloomingdale Sanitorium, a private hospital, for a lengthy treatment. In her absence, Louis tried to economize by moving the family to an inexpensive apartment near his school in Paterson. About the time that Allen was beginning school at the age of five, Naomi was released from the sanitarium. Bloomingdale had been expensive, and as a result Louis had been forced to borrow heavily from the local credit union, but for a while it all seemed to have been worthwhile. For the next four or five years Naomi remained somewhat stable and they had high hopes for the future. Every summer the family would alternate vacations between the New Jersey shore with Louis' family (which Naomi did not en-

Mendel Livergant, Eugene, Allen, Naomi, and Louis Ginsberg, ca. 1936

joy) and communist camps in upstate New York (her preference). Occasionally she and Louis visited a communist-run nudist camp in the Catskills.

Allen remembered going to camps like Camp Nicht-Gedeigat (Yiddish for "no worries"), a communist-run retreat near Lake Monroe, NY. The children played the usual outdoor games and explored the surrounding woods, while the parents engaged in vigorous political debates. They went to Nicht-Gedeigat at least twice and occasionally another camp near Indian Point in Woodstock, NY. In order to keep up with his loan payments, Louis taught summer school and joined the family on the weekends.

This period of relative calm lasted for about five years, though Louis had financial difficulties, exacerbated by the Great

Depression, which had forced the school district to cut his salary by one third. He bristled when Naomi criticized him for being unsuccessful and having no money, it was her hospitalization that had caused their debt. They quarreled over other things, too, such as her nudity in front of the boys: Louis felt that she did it more to irritate him than from any dedication to naturalism.

Then in 1935, Naomi had another attack of hypersensitivity. This time she spent the better part of two months in a darkened room in their apartment. When she suffered another attack a few months later, Louis had to send her away again. The family could no longer afford a private sanitarium, and Naomi was committed to Greystone Hospital, a state-run facility near Morristown. During her stay there, she received nearly forty insulin shock treatments, the standard treatment for patients with paranoid schizophrenia. The doctors at Greystone also administered Metrazol, a drug used to stimulate circulation and respiration in convulsive therapy. It was common then, but later it was shown that Metrazol provided few positive results for patients. It did, however, have many negative side-effects, one of which was to radically change Naomi's appearance. She came out of the hospital bloated and overweight. Allen mentioned in his diary that she was now "very fat, lost her girlish laughter and figure." During this stay in the hospital, Naomi began to hallucinate and imagined that the doctors had implanted wires and sticks in her back for the purpose of controlling her.

The following summer, she was released from Greystone and the family tried to put on a happy face and return to their normal routine. For a bit of relaxation, they rented a summer cottage in Woodstock, NY, and Naomi's father visited. Their place was within a few blocks of town and Naomi participated in the annual Village Fair, where she won first prize for the most beautiful homemade dress. It

Naomi, Allen and Louis Ginsberg at the New York World's Fair, 1940

was as idyllic a summer as the family had ever had. Allen remembered that there were very few fights between his parents, but that when they returned to Paterson the arguments resumed. As a rule their fights began over money, but soon they would develop into heated shouting matches. It was during this period that Naomi taunted Louis with stories of her alleged affairs with Maxwell Bodenheim and others.

On June 24, 1937, she slashed her wrists in a suicide attempt in their small apartment. Allen, eleven years old at the time, had stayed home from school to keep an eye on her, while Louis went to work. In the morning she locked herself in the bathroom, and Louis had to be called home to break down the door. He found Naomi covered in blood and the next morning she was taken by ambulance back to Greystone. That summer Allen and Eugene were sent to the Jersey shore to stay with the Ginsberg family. Naomi was institutionalized for two years, released only for occasional weekends and holidays.

By now the pattern was established. Naomi was committed to mental hospitals for longer and longer periods, only to be released and returned again, her mind gradually growing more and more confused. She did have productive intervals, and while Allen attended high school classes in Paterson, Naomi managed to write and publish a few short, parable-like stories in the *Paterson Press*. She also enjoyed playing the piano when she was at home, but she could never be alone without supervision.

When Naomi returned to Paterson in the fall of 1939, after a period of relative quiet at the sanitarium, she walked into her apartment and went directly to bed. For the rest of the day Allen stayed beside her. She assured him that she had recovered. For nearly two years she remained relatively peaceful until her paranoid fears about Louis and Grandmother Buba took over once again. In the winter of 1941 she suffered another seizure and fled to the bathroom. Allen found her there covered in vomit and feces, an image he never forgot. She begged him to help her escape from Louis' clutches. Allen, fifteen at the time, hoped that her physician would be able to help, and he called Dr. Hans Wassing, who suggested that Allen take Naomi to a private rest home in Lakewood, NJ, a few hours away by bus. By the time they arrived in Lakewood, Naomi was so out of control that the rest home would not admit her. She and Allen then walked to another nursing home nearby that did agree to accept her. Allen returned to Paterson that night and told a stunned Louis what had happened. Louis could not believe that his son had taken such a risk and he knew it would not be the end of the matter. In the middle of the night they received a phone call from Lakewood

Naomi Ginsberg, ca. 1930s

telling them that Naomi had gone completely berserk. The next day, still not wanting to send her back to the mental hospital, Louis hired an ambulance to transport her to Hillgreen, a rest home in Passaic. But within a week Naomi was back at Greystone.

She stayed there for more than a year this time, trying to regain her mental balance. When she was released, she rejoined Louis, but by this time their marriage was beyond repair. They separated in 1943, soon to divorce, and Naomi moved to New York City. Her fantasy world persisted. She was certain that Louis and his mother were still trying to kill her. She imagined that they brought poisonous bugs into the house to throw on her; she suspected they were in league with Hitler and Roosevelt, out to get her; she felt that she was being controlled by wires and sticks in her back. Naomi's sister,

Elanor, who lived with her husband in the Bronx, tried to help her get settled. She found Naomi a job addressing envelopes at the Workman's Circle and then introduced her to a Communist Party activist named Leon Luria. Dr. Luria was the staff physician for the National Maritime Union and had an office on West 18th Street near union headquarters. Naomi worked as his receptionist for a short time and became his lover. She moved in with him, but slept on the sofa in his office when she wanted to be alone. While she was living with Luria, Allen was accepted into Columbia College and had his mail delivered to Naomi's 18th Street address.

Naomi's relationship with Dr. Luria did not last long. She began to believe that Luria was in league with Louis and Buba, so by 1946 she had left him. She tried living for a brief time with her son Eugene, and then moved back to the Bronx. This time she roomed with Elanor's sister-in-law, Edith (Edie) Frohman, who worked as a union organizer at Gimbels department store and lived in Elanor's building. Edie and Naomi attended Communist Party meetings together, took political petitions door to door, and frequented rallies and lectures. Naomi enrolled at an adult high school in the Bronx for evening classes in art, where she painted some wonderful pictures.

After a while, the inevitable happened, and Naomi took another turn for the worse. She began to imagine that Grandma Buba's spies had taken over the radio. Then she imagined that she saw the old woman climbing the fire escape, lugging a bag of poison germs. Naomi became increasingly violent and continually kicked Elanor, who already suffered from rheumatic heart disease. Even Edie became a spy and a rat in her delusional state of mind. One evening it all became too much to bear and Allen was called as a last resort. He spent a long time trying to calm his mother and talk rationally to her, assuring her that there were no wires in her back, no secret radio in the ceiling, and that Buba was too old to hurt her. But Naomi was beyond reason and insisted that her enemies were smarter than he was. Finally, Allen gave up and called the police himself. This time Naomi was taken to Pilgrim State Hospital for treatment.

Months later, during the summer of 1949, the doctors at Pilgrim State released Naomi and she asked Allen if she could move in with him. But Allen was in no position to take care of anyone at that point in his life. He had recently been arrested for permitting Herbert Huncke and two other petty criminals to store stolen merchandise in his apartment. Allen pled guilty, and instead of being sent to prison he was sent to the New York State Psychiatric Hospital. Allen believed that he might be on the verge of insanity, too, given his mother's mental history. With nowhere to turn, Naomi quickly found herself back in Pilgrim State.

The doctors at Pilgrim State were experimenting with a new surgical procedure for treating patients who were violent or self-destructive and, in November Allen received a letter asking for his permission to perform a prefrontal lobotomy on Naomi. (Louis and Naomi had recently divorced, and Louis no longer had a say in her treatment.) Allen Reluctantly agreed, hoping the surgery would help calm her troubled mind. Unfortunately, the operation failed to alleviate her paranoia; she never recovered from the trauma and withdrew into herself, afraid of everything and everyone. She was a ward of the state for the remainder of her life.

Allen would visit Naomi at the hospital from time to time, but she increasingly failed to recognize him. On January 18, 1953, Allen visited Naomi for what might have been the last time. She was frightened and didn't recognize him and soon asked the attendant to take her back to her room. Allen cried as this final curtain was drawn between mother and son.

Late in 1953, Allen left New York, traveling for months through Mexico before arriving in San Francisco where he found a job, met his life's companion Peter Orlovsky, and began writing the poems which would eventually make him famous. It was while he was working on the proofs of *Howl and Other Poems* that he received the telegram from his father telling him that Naomi had died from a stroke on June 9, 1956.

Her body was laid out in a funeral parlor in Hempstead, Long Island, and only seven people attended her funeral the following day. She was buried in Beth Moses Cemetery in Farmingdale, not far from the hospital where she had spent her final years. Allen's brother Eugene described it to him in a letter, "The day was nice and sunny. 7 people: Lou, Abe and Anna [Ginsberg], Eugene, Max Frohman, Connie Brooks and Fanny Freiman [or Frieman?], Naomi's high school chum. . . . We saw the body briefly—she was quite recognizable—her face was perhaps a little sad, although in repose." While they were there they visited the grave of her sister Elanor, who was buried about a hundred yards away. No one had ever told Naomi that her sister was dead, or that her continual physical and verbal abuse might have hastened her death.

A little more than a week later, Louis wrote to Allen, "It is difficult to write you and tell in a few words a life-full of love for Naomi. Though Fate had severed her physically from me for the last few years, I confess she was in my heart always. There was no day during which I was in a crowd or happy that thoughts of Naomi, torn within herself and cooped up in a desolate room, did not invade my mind. As I saw her coffin lowered into the hospitable earth, I thought that now she would at last have peace and rest, something I had struggled all my life in vain to give her."

Although that might seem like the end of the story for Naomi, it is only half of the tale. Harvey Shapiro, in his 1961 review of *Kaddish and Other Poems* commented that Naomi might be forever remembered as "the most bizarre muse in English Lit." Although "bizarre" seems a harsh word, there is some truth in what he said. Never was there such an unlikely heroine in modern poetry. She suffered a lifetime of mental breakdowns, suicide attempts, and a lobotomy to inspire one of the great works of the twentieth century. Although Allen used her tragic story as the inspiration for his greatest poem, Naomi was first and foremost a cherished mother, someone he loved without reservation. The poem itself was destined to become, as Robert Lowell declared, "a terrible masterpiece."

The Story of "Kaddish"

A week or so after Naomi's death, Allen left San Francisco harbor on board the USNS *Jack J. Pendleton.* He wrote to his brother Eugene telling him that he had been thinking about nothing but Naomi and death. "We all die," he said, "life's a short flash." He stood on the prow of the ship facing into the roaring sea with the full force of the wind in his face and realized there was a "great majesty and tenderness to life, a kind of instantaneous universal joy at creation." When he passed through the Bering Straits, close to the Russian coast, the country where Naomi had been born, he threw a few coins into the water in her memory. He wrote to his grandmother, Buba Ginsberg, promising to go to Russia someday and visit any relatives that might still be living there. "Naomi's death made me remember my own generation, and how it must pass," he said. For his entire adult life, Allen had been fixated on death, and his mother's passing only increased his desire to unlock its mysteries.

When he returned from his assignment in Alaska on July 10,

Allen was surprised to find a letter from his mother waiting for him. The letter had been written just a few days before her death, and a well-meaning hospital worker must have dropped it in the mail. It was by far the most lucid statement he had received from her in years. She counseled him with motherly advice, urging him to find a job and get married. She warned him about the dangers of alcohol "and other things that are not good for you." It came as a voice from beyond the grave. Her last words to him were: "Don't go in for ridiculous things." He wept for himself and for the mother he had lost long before her death.

By the end of the month, Allen's ship was back in the Arctic. Lying on his bunk on the morning of July 29, 1956, he noted in his journal, "Kaddish or the Sea Poem, irregular lines each perfect. Now all is changed for me, as all is changed for thee, Naomi." He ended with a note to himself, "Write Kaddish." It was an idea that would ripen in his mind for more than a year before he would get back to it. For the present, he wanted to know more about the Kaddish, since he had not been raised a practicing Jew. He wrote to Louis and asked him for a copy of the prayer. In August his father wrote back saying, "I just called up a friend who will procure the Kaddish in Hebrew and English so I shall dispatch it to you shortly."

Immediately following Naomi's death, both Eugene and Louis went to work on beautiful poems in her memory. On August 13, 1956, Allen's father wrote to him, "Yes, Eugene's poem, as I told him, was one of his best. His lines caught commingled pathos and heartbreak. I myself am working on half a dozen lyrics about Naomi's funeral, as it affected me."

In the course of the next year, Allen stopped off in Paterson to visit his father and stepmother on his way to Europe. He was funded by a small inheritance of $1,000 that Naomi had left him, saved over the last few years from her meager allowance. In Paris during November 1957, he hung out at places on the Left Bank like the Cafe Select, sipping coffee and writing poetry. One of the requiems he composed was what he called a "long elegy for mama." Later he would say of this poem, "I see [it as] one big frightened hang-up about my own death which is what all the mournful hysteric poetry is all about." He worked on sections of a final poem he called the "lament litany and fugue parts." It began with the lines "Farewell | with long black shoe | Farewell | smoking corsets & ribs of steel . . ." Allen worked on this version of the poem throughout the late fall and into the early winter, adding fragments to it from time to time. But he was unable to find the right form and style, and finally, set it aside.

Another year was to pass before he got back to his long poem about his mother, which still hadn't quite taken shape in his mind. In mid-November 1958, he found himself back in New York City, this time living in a cheap apartment with Peter Orlovsky. He had been thinking about his poem for his mother a great deal, without putting anything on paper. William Carlos Williams had been encouraging him to write shorter "prose seed" poems, based on imagistic notations from his diaries, but Allen wanted to expand on that idea. He felt that at the heart of Williams' work was the desire to find poetic measure in the careful observation of normal, everyday speech. "What if you observe abnormally excited speech, wailing, crying, as at mother deathbed or moments of extreme emotional stress?" he wrote to Charles Olson. "You'll find various archetype real fixed rhythms to work with poetically and build huge structures on." Allen had done this in "Howl," and was now ready to carry it even further with his "mother poem." It was to be an experiment. It might never amount to anything, but he was eager to get started.

One night Allen was hanging out with his friend, Zev Putterman who lived on the other side of town. Zev had a number of Ray Charles albums, and as the two listened to the records, Allen read parts of Shelley's "Adonaïs" aloud. Gregory Corso had been encouraging Allen to study Shelley more carefully, and it inspired him to think of poetry in elegiac and heroic terms. During the course of the night he tried some morphine and a bit of methamphetamine for the very first time. It gave him the energy to continue talking into the wee hours of the morning. He asked Putterman to read him the Kaddish, since he couldn't read Hebrew himself and as he walked back home to the East Village, the rhythms of the prayer resounded in his head.

At some point, he realized that he was walking down the same streets his mother had known as a little girl, only just arrived from Russia. As soon as he got to his apartment, he sat down at his desk and began to write. Starting first by describing the walk across town, he used it as a reference point for the beginning of the story of Naomi's life. He employed the same long line narrative style he had used in "Howl," but this time he paid even more attention to the rhythm of the words. He thought of the poem as a Bach fugue, building the emotions in words instead of musical notes. He wrote quickly, making breaks only to show where one thought stopped and another began. For the next day and a half he sat at his desk writing. When the blue ballpoint pen he was using ran out of ink he grabbed another from his desk, a red one, and continued for fifty-eight pages of dense handwritten verse. He cried as he wrote, tears streaming down his cheeks.

When he was finished, Allen put the pages in his desk drawer and slept soundly for the first time in days. He had been so desperate to capture his feeling while he had the inspiration and energy to do it; when he awoke he almost couldn't remember what he had written. At first he was undecided about the poem and wasn't even certain it was poetry. He dared not open the desk drawer for a week, afraid that what he had created might be nothing more than exhausted scribbles. Later he recalled, "When I reread the mass I was defeated, it seemed impossible to clean up and revise."

He was also afraid of what his friends and family would think. He knew what he had written might potentially "cause distress or anxiety" to several people. It was one thing to write a long confessional poem for yourself, but quite another to confront his father with his version of Naomi's tragic life. It was certain to dredge up feelings and memories that Louis might prefer to forget. Once again he put the manuscript aside. In the coming months he would return to it and rework small sections, but it would be nearly a year before he sat down to tackle the entire manuscript again.

Unlike "Howl," which he re-typed soon after composition and sent out in excerpts to friends like Kerouac, Allen kept the manuscript of "Kaddish" to himself for a long time. He would occasionally mention the fact that he had written a long poem in a burst of energy, but he was reluctant to share it with anyone. Eventually, in the spring of 1959, he sent a few fragments of the poem to his father for his opinion. With only minor reservations his father wrote back enthusiastically. "It is nostalgic and poignant; some lines are heartwrenching, what with not only you but me being at that time in the middle of the anguish. Some of the lines are poetically magnificent and imaginatively vivid."

Lawrence Ferlinghetti had been asking Ginsberg for his next collection of poetry. After the success of *Howl and Other Poems*, which Lawrence had published in the fall of 1956 and defended in court during the summer of 1957, Ferlinghetti was ready to publish his next book. By the time Allen wrote "Kaddish," a remarkable 30,000 copies of *Howl and Other Poems* were in print. Ginsberg had become famous enough to demand a big advance from a large New York publisher, but he chose to remain with City Lights out of loyalty to the man who had been arrested for publishing his work. Ginsberg suggested that they proceed slowly with this next book. He wanted it to be stronger than *Howl and Other Poems* and he knew that it would take time to put the collection into the shape he wanted. "*Howl* still sells so why rush?" he replied to Ferlinghetti's urging.

On February 5, 1959, Ginsberg gave his first reading of parts of the recently completed poem at Columbia University. His father was in the audience to listen and both father and son wept; at one point Allen had to pause in his reading to regain his composure. Louis had been disturbed by some of the extremely detailed and personal things about the family that Allen had revealed in the poem. He questioned Allen's use of vocabulary when describing the "hair around the vagina" and disliked the fact that Allen mentioned his own "mountains of homosexuality," something that Louis still must have hoped was merely a temporary state. After hearing the poem read aloud to the 1,400 people who packed the McMillan Auditorium that night, Louis agreed with Allen's decision to speak honestly from the heart, avoiding self-censorship, but he still did not condone the use of "dirty words."

After the overwhelming ovation for the poem, Allen was more confident that he'd created something worthwhile. Although he considered it a strange mixture amounting to half prose and half poetry, he was as proud of the work as he would ever be of anything he wrote. The staccato phrasing was meant to elicit the same sobbing from the listener as it did from the poet. The rhythm builds through-out the poem into an ecstatic climax, and when it was read aloud, the harmony of the words became apparent. Ferlinghetti, great editor that he is, suggested that Allen shorten the poem somewhat and tighten it in places. Allen took his advice, but then began to have second thoughts and felt that maybe he'd shortened it too much

The final page of "Kaddish," the "caw caw caw" segment, was the last section that Allen tackled. Written in the winter of 1959, it was based on his first visit to Naomi's grave. At the time he made note of the screeching of the crows who had been disturbed by his presence in the quiet cemetery. They reminded him of the crows in Van Gogh's final painting, *Wheatfield with Crows*, and Poe's symbolic raven, another ominous symbol of death. The repetitive sounds became an important climax to a poem that was built orally line by line, ever increasing in intensity and emotion. Now, using purely sound, instead of words, he brought the poem to its proper conclusion in a wail of remorse.

Still he wasn't quite ready to do anything with his poem. It still needed a lot of work to condense and tighten some of the lengthier passages. In 1960 Ginsberg went on a trip to South America for a writer's conference that turned into a six months escape in the Amazon jungle. Initially on a search for yagé, the hallucinogenic plant that William Burroughs had described to him as the "death vine," he found a native shaman to administer the drug safely. Allen believed he had come as close to experiencing death as he ever would. That visitation with death was the final impetus he needed to complete "Kaddish." When he returned to his apartment in New York, he sat down once again at his typewriter. On the afternoon of September 14, Allen began his second marathon session with the manuscript. Aided only by an occasional bit of benzedrine and dexedrine to energize him, he revised the poem one last time. Almost immediately he began to weep. "I write best when I cry," he pointed out. "Some kind of tenderness shining thru tears." Later he wrote, "Sometimes this appears to be divine inspiration—I get the feeling, it's an ecstatic lucidity, that the world can be entered and prophesied to by a single soul, alone." The revision of "Kaddish" was a major undertaking and although parts were kept intact, many parts were completely eliminated or re-written. The whole "Hymmnn" section was substantially shortened, for example. "I sat down at desk 3 PM last Wednesday and did not rise except to pee till 9 PM Thursday nite, having typed up complete 'Kaddish' mss. Adding various Shelleyan Hymns written in sobracked exhausted trances, and took it to 33rd St. post office to mail to Ferlinghetti special delivery Sat. nite at 4 AM, that's done." He also mailed a copy to his father, knowing that would be the real litmus test of the poem's ability to capture the essence of Naomi's life.

In October 1960 he read it aloud to an enthusiastic Jack Kerouac, the only person whose literary opinion he truly valued, and finally was satisfied with the results. "It sounded foursquare and right what I want," he told Ferlinghetti. "I take back earlier doubt as to whether it should be published." From that moment on he never doubted that it was his masterpiece.

Ferlinghetti was enthusiastic. This was exactly the kind of poem he hoped to publish as a follow-up to "Howl." He insisted that Allen get releases from his father and brother, however, sensing just how revealing the work was. Eugene had no real objections about the poem as a poem. He did feel that Allen was telling his own story, and that it was not necessarily the same story that Eugene himself might tell. Louis once more strongly suggested that Allen delete the description of the "long black beard around vagina", a phrase that he considered "too obscene for reference to mother." He had noted the same in the earlier excerpt he had read. He also reminded Allen to remove his references to homosexuality. "You'll invite slander, irrelevant to literary merits." Allen replied to him almost immediately, taking issue with most of what he had to say. He felt that other people had similar experiences with family members and that it was only because Louis was so close to the subject that he was offended. In the end the vagina and homosexual revelations remained.

Allen agreed to remove the references he had made to the fact that Louis was having a love affair during the years he was married to Naomi. "The dentist's wife writes love letters to Lou," Allen had revealed. There was no need to embarrass Louis and it was not central to the point of the poem. His father also questioned another long section in the poem, in which Allen described a childhood masturbation episode. Allen remembered that he had rubbed against his father's leg one night in bed, but Louis had no memory of that and could not understand why Allen would want to bring that up. That section was deleted without further comment.

The first edition of *Kaddish and Other Poems* was published by Ferlinghetti in February 1961 in a small edition of 2,500 copies, which took nearly three years to sell out. Since then however, the book has enjoyed a steady increase in sales as the public has slowly come to realize the importance of the work contained in that slim volume. In the years that followed nearly 200,000 copies of the book have been printed.

As Allen's friend Elise Cowen noted, as she helped him type up the final manuscript, " You still haven't finished with your mother." It turned out she was right. This book was not to be the end of Allen's obsession with his mother, or the end of the creative work her memory inspired. When Allen returned from two years in India in 1963, he was broke and unsure about how he might earn a living. Fortunately, the photographer Robert Frank stepped in with

Portrait of Allen Ginsberg, *painting by Naomi Ginsberg, ca 1947*

COURTESY OF ALLEN GINSBERG TRUST

an idea. Robert had read "Kaddish" and considered it great film material. He employed Allen to write a cinematic script based on the poem and paid him $10 an hour, which was enough to pay the bills until his next royalty check arrived from City Lights. Allen regarded this as a subsidy gratefully received, and he was only sorry that the film itself never materialized; as with many film projects, Frank was unable to find backers willing to invest, and the project never got beyond the filmscript stage. In the meantime, Robert Frank began to film a low-budget movie about Peter Orlovsky and his brother. That film eventually became the underground classic, *Me and My Brother,* and so Allen felt that something worthwhile did ultimately result from his efforts.

In 1972, the idea of performing "Kaddish" as a drama was revived again, this time in the form of a stage production. The play was presented by Robert Kalfin for New York's Chelsea Theater and later moved to the Circle in the Square, where it received some very good reviews, including a rave from Clive Barnes, the *New York*

Times' powerful theater critic. Later, in 1977, NET adapted "Kaddish" for television as a narrated version of the poem. Since then various groups have performed "Kaddish," including a memorable off-off-Broadway version with set designs by the artist Eric Fischl. Allen himself wasn't done with Naomi's memory either. She appeared again as the inspiration for both his poems, "White Shroud' in 1983 and 'Black Shroud' in 1984.

Until the day he died, Ginsberg was still trying to unravel the mysteries of suffering and death, and his mother remained his primary example of the unexplainable sadness of life. He studied Buddhist philosophy hoping to unlock the secrets of life, and over time came to believe that there was no answer to any of life's great questions. As regards the legacy that we have inherited from Allen Ginsberg through his mother's story in "Kaddish," perhaps Ezra Pound stated it best, "Only emotion endures."

Bill Morgan

HOW KADDISH HAPPENED

Editor's Note: Perhaps the best overview of the creation of the poem was written by Allen himself in 1966 as the liner notes for his Atlantic Records recording of Kaddish.

First writing on "Kaddish" was in Paris '58, several pages of part IV which set forth a new variation on the litany form used earlier in "Howl"—a graduated lengthening of the response lines, so that the "Howl "litany looks like a big pyramid on the page. "Kaddish IV" looks like three little pyramids sitting one on top of another, plus an upside-down pyramid mirror– reflected at the bottom of the series. Considered as breath, it means the vocal reader has to build up the feeling-utterance three times to climax, and then, as coda, diminish the utterance to shorter and shorter sob. The first mess of composition had all these elements, I later cut it down to look neat and exact.

Sometime a year later in New York I sat up all night with a friend who played me Ray Charles' genius classics—I'd been in Europe two winters and not heard attentively before—also we chippied a little M [morphine] and some then new-to-me meta-amphetamine—friend showed me his old bar-mitzvah book of Hebrew ritual and read me central Kaddish passages—I walked out in early blue dawn on to 7th Avenue and across town to my Lower East Side apartment—New York before sunrise has its own celebrated hallucinatory unreality. In the country getting up with the cows and birds hath Blakean charm, in the megalopolis the same nature's hour is a science-fiction hell vision, even if you're a milkman. Phantom factories, unpopulated streets out of Poe, familiar nightclubs bookstores groceries dead.

I got home and sat at desk with desire to write—a kind of visionary urge that's catalyzed by all the strange chemicals of the city—but had no idea what Prophecy was at hand—poetry I figured. I began quite literally assembling recollection data taken from the last hours—"Strange now to think of you gone without corsets and eyes while I walk etc." I wrote on several pages till I'd reached a climax, covering fragmentary recollections of key scenes with my mother ending with a death-prayer imitating the rhythms of the Hebrew Kaddish—"Magnificent, Mourned no more, etc."

But then I realized that I hadn't gone back and told the whole secret family-self tale—my own one-and-only eternal child-youth memories which no one else could know—in all its eccentric detail. I realized that it would seem odd to others, but *family* odd, that is to say, familiar—everybody has crazy cousins and aunts and brothers.

So I started over again into narrative—"This is release of particulars"—and went back chronologically sketching in broken paragraphs all the first recollections that rose in my heart—details I'd thought of once, twice, often before—embarrassing scenes I'd half amnesiaized—hackle-raising scenes of the long black beard around the vagina—images that were central of scars on my mother's plump belly—all archetypes.

Possibly subjective archetypes, but archetype is archetype, and properly articulated subjective archetype is universal.

I sat at same desk from 6 AM Saturday to ten PM Sunday night writing on without moving my mind from theme except for trips to the bathroom, cups of coffee and boiled egg handed into my room by Peter Orlovsky (Peter the nurse watching over his beloved madman) and a few Dexedrine tablets to renew impulse. After the twentieth hour attention wandered, the writing became more diffuse, dissociations more difficult to cohere, the unworldly messianic spurts more awkward, but I persevered till completing the chronological task. I got the last detail recorded including my mother's death-telegram. I could go back later and clean it up.

I didn't look at the handwritten pages for a week—slept several days—and when I re-read the mass I was defeated, it seemed impossible to clean up and revise, the continuous impulse was there messy as it was, it was a patient scholar's task to figure how it could be more shapely.

Standing on a streetcorner one dusk another variation of the litany form came to me—alternation of Lord Lord and Caw Caw ending with a line of pure Lord Lord Lord Caw Caw Caw— pure emotive sound—and I went home and filled in that form with associational data. The last three lines are among the best in the poem—the *most* dissociated, on the surface, but, given all the detail of the poem, quite coherent—I mean it's a very great jump from the broken shoe to the last highschool caw caw—and in that gap's the whole Maya-Dream-Suchness of existence glimpsed.

It took me a year—trip to South America half that time—to have the patience to type poem up so I could read it. I delayed, depressed with the mess, not sure it was a poem. Much less interesting to anyone else. Defeat like that is good for poetry—you go so far out you don't know what you're doing, you lose touch with what's been done before by anyone, you wind up creating a new poetry-universe. "Make it new" saith Pound, "Invention," said William Carlos Williams. That's the "Tradition"—a complete fuck-up so you're on your own.

The poem was typed, I had to cut down and stitch together the last sections of narrative—didn't have to change the expression, but did have to fit it together where it lapsed into abstract bathos or got mixed in time or changed track too often. [. . .]

Allen Ginsberg

of failure. Blessed be you Naomi of Hospitals!
Blessed, Blessed, Blessed be you Naomi of Death!
Dead by you, Naomi in Tears. Blessed
in Tears. Blessed in Hopes. Blessed in
Longing. Blessed in Vision! Blessed in
Sadness! Blessed in Motherhood! Blessed
in Naomi! Blessed be thy Mandoline!
Blest be thy Triumph! Blest be thy Bars
Blest by your last years loneliness! Blest
be you in Jehova! Blessed be He! Blessed
Be He!

Blessed be Naomi, in Death where she is.
Blessed be Death! Blessed be Death!

Blest be Naomi in memory! Blest be in
Death! Blessed be Death!

Blest be my poem to Naomi! Blest in
its failure! Blest in Naomi! Blessed be He!

Blessed be Naomi in Heaven, Blessed
be Heaven, Blessed be Death Blessed be Death!

her death! Blest be her Shock! Blest be
Lobotomy! Blest be her Stroke! Blest be the
Close of her eye! Blest be the gaunt of her
Cheek! Blest be the withered-thigh! Blest
be her failing of Truth! Blest be her
Sorrow! Blessed be He

Blessed be he

who leads alle sorrow to Heaven
Blessed be He

Who'll lead Naomi to Heaven

Blessed be Heaven Blessed be Heaven

Blessed be He who builds heaven in Darkness

Blessed be He! Blessed be He!

Blessed be Death for Naomi! Blessed

be Naomi in Death

Blessed, Farewell, o death! o Naomi!
Blessed be He! Blessed be thee!

Blessed be Death on us all!

Allen Ginsberg's "Kaddish," is widely considered to be his finest poem. This special fiftieth-anniversary edition features a new afterword by noted Ginsberg biographer Bill Morgan, along with family photographs, facsimile pages from the original manuscript, and Allen Ginsberg's illuminating essay, "How Kaddish Happened."

In the midst of the broken consciousness of mid twentieth century suffering anguish of separation from my own body and its natural infinity of feeling its own self one with all self, I instinctively seeking to reconstitute that blissful union which I experienced so rarely I took it to be supernatural and gave it a holy Name thus made hymn laments of longing and litanies of triumphancy of Self over the mind-illusion mechano-universe of un-feeling Time in which I saw my self my own mother and my very nation trapped desolate our worlds of consciousness homeless and at war except for the original trembling of bliss in breast and belly of every body that nakedness rejected in suits of fear that familiar defenseless living hurt self which is myself same as all others abandoned scared to own our unchanging desire for each other. These poems almost un-conscious to confess the beatific human fact, the language intui-tively chosen as in trance & dream, the rhythms rising on breath from belly thru breast, the hymn completed in tears, the movement of the physical poetry demanding and receiving decades of life while chanting Kaddish the name of Death in many mind-worlds the self seeking the Key to life found at last in our self.

ALLEN GINSBERG.

$12.95
ISBN 978-0-87286-511-2
51295>

9 780872 865112